GANDHI AND ANARCHY

GANDHI AND ANARCHY

By

SIR C. SANKARAN NAIR

GYAN

Published by

GYAN

Gyan Publishing House
5, Ansari Road
Daryaganj, New Delhi-110002
Phone: 011-47034999, 9811692060
E-mail: books@gyanbooks.com

Distribution Network
gyanbooks.com
India, USA, Canada, UK, Australia, France

ISBN : 978-81-212-6703-8 (PB)
First Published, 1922

2nd Impression 2022

Printed at: Gyan Press, Delhi.

GANDHI AND ANARCHY

Author: Sir C. Sankaran Nair

GANDHI AND ANARCHY

By

SIR C. SANKARAN NAIR

CONTENTS

PREFACE

The struggle for Indian Home Rule which was started with the inauguration of the Indian National Congress has many difficulties to encounter, has strong and powerful opponents and has received many checks. But its strongest opponent is Mr. Gandhi and perhaps the most severe check it has received is the adoption by the National Congress at his instance in Calcutta and Nagpur of the so-called-Non-violent Non-co-operation. Non-co-operation as advocated by Mr. Gandhi may be a weapon to be used when constitutional methods have failed to achieve our purpose. Non-violence and passive suffering will lead to bloodshed or be unfruitful of any satisfactory results. Moreover, nothing shows the lack of statesmanship more than practically basing the claim for Swaraj upon the Punjab and the Khilafat grievances. As representing Asia against Europe, the fair against the white race, the Hindus regarded the Turkish Empire with sympathy and were disposed to support the Mahomadens as Asiatic representatives. But when by Gandhi and Khilafatist that claim was abandoned ; when the Arabs perhaps the noblest of the Mahomadan races who fought as our allies and helped us to defeat Turkey were sought to be brought under Turkish dominion, when other Asiatic races freed by the war were asked to accept Turkish Soveriegnty on grounds based on the Mahomaden religion which had already produced such baneful result in India, the situation became entirely different. It was rightly realised by many, and the sequel has proved that they were right that the path of the progress of the Gandhi movement fused with the Khilafat element will be bloody. The claim for Indian Home Rule rests upon very different grounds. The Hindus have nothing to do with the Khilafat agitation. The Mahomadans themselves are not agreed as to the claims advanced on behalf of the Calif It is even questionable, to put it mildly, whether that claim has the support of the majority of the Mahomadans. While the claim itself rested on such slender grounds, the means first adopted to enforce the claim were grotesque. The methods advocated by Mr. Gandhi and the Congress are directed against Western civilization; against the class which fought for and won the reforms; and the Montague reforms scheme of constitutional progress. They have failed miserably and as was natural more violent methods leading to direct conflict with the forces of Government have been advocated which would in all probability have been carried out but for the arrest and imprisonment of Mr. Gandhi. He belongs to a class of thought which has attracted some of the noblest minds in this world, but in applying his the gospel of life to politics, he has shown himself a babe and his interference has been generally mischievous. In South Africa he is responsible for creating a situation which makes a peaceful and satisfactory solution practically impossible. His factious policy in India stands in the way of further reforms. The opposition to Gandhi was however not strenous. The so-called Moderates only whispered their protests against his policy so as not to be heard beyond a few feet. They are loud however, in their denunciation of Government action to check the illegal activities of Mr.

Gandhi and his followers. It can hardly be doubted that their cautious attitude has contributed to the growth of the Gandhi movement. But the inexplicable conduct of a certain—I won't say class—body of gentlemen has still more contributed to that result.

There is scracely any item in the Gandhi programme which is not a complete violation of everything preached by the foremost sons of India till 1919; which has not been strongly even vehemently denounced by those old respected members of the Congress who now follow Mr. Gandhi, Pandit Malaviya, Messrs. Vijayaragavachari, Lajapat Rai, Natarajam, S. Kasturiranga Iyengar, the Editor of the 'Hindu.' Mr. Gandhi's emotional outbursts, fastings, penances, Sanyasi waist cloth, may carry away the emotional masses, women and students. But whether this wave of emotionalism submerged the men abovenamed I would not care to guess. No one of course has any right to find fault with his genuine followers like Mr. Prakasam, Editor, 'Swaraj' whose motives, however much we might differ from his politics, no one will question. He is one of those genuine patriots who believes in the efficacy of Mr. Gandhi's methods to obtain

Home Rule. By far the great majority however, follow him for other reasons.

The severe simplicity and austerity of Mr. Gandhi's life combined with his appeal to the principle of '*Ahimsa*' non-injury inherited from Buddists and now ingrained in Hindu life, has secured him the support of the Hindu masses and particularly vegetarians. His support of the caste system has won over the higher classes and the reactionary elements of Hindu society to his side. The caste system is entirely opposed to the 'Ahimsa' (Non-injury) principle. The former has dedicated one of the main castes to death. Its function is to kill and be killed. It is also the function of some of the sub-castes of the lowest caste or class to slaughter animals. His indiscriminating support of the extreme Khilafat demands has ensured the Mahomedan support. Islam is more opposed than the caste system to "Ahimsa." The trouble with the Hindus over the slaughter of cows is due to this difficulty. Some politicians who naturally desire to use him and the influence he has acquired for putting pressure on the Government to concede further reform, also have joined him. But I am satisfied he is using them all to further his own ends. An attempt in which he is bound to fail. His success *i. e.* the success of the reactionary forces in India to obtain what they call Dominion status or Home Rule, but, which really means their rule, will not only lead to bloodshed and anarchy and the dismemberment of the Empire ; but to the triumph of a reactionary policy, social, moral and economic, against which the democratic policy of the recent reforms and the Legislative Councils is an emphatic protest. I have attempted in the following pages to give my reasons for these conclusions.

Far more important than my narrative are the extracts published in the appendix. They consist of speeches made by the Viceroy, and members of Government in the Legislative Councils. I have on account of considerations of space omitted speeches in many provinces. I have not given any speech in full for the same reason. I have also given a list of riots or disturbances. These give a fair idea of the activities of Mr. Gandhi.

C. SANKARAN NAIR

GANDHI AND ANARCHY

HIS PHILOSOPHY

ALL of us are now striving for "Swaraj" or Home Rule. We wish to be masters of our own destiny. We want sooner or later the representatives of the people of the country to govern it. There are some amongst us who consider that Home Rule, is an immediate necessity. Others believe that Home Rule, at present without the fulfilment of certain preliminary conditions would be attended with disastrous results. But all are agreed that we should work for it. The practical difficulties in the way of its attainment due, partly to the relations between the various communities in India, partly to the opposition of powerful interests and the period that must therefore elapse before we overcome them render the discussion of time, ignoring or brushing aside those difficulties, only of acadamic interest. Mr. Gandhi's great influence is due to the popular belief in the efficacy of his leadership to attain immediate Home Rule. To me his Non-Copera-tion Campaign appears to be an egregious blunder for which we are already paying dearly. A long line of illustrious statesmen, Indian and English have just succeeded in leading us out of the house of bondage. How long we shall have to wander in the deserts we do not know. But it is certain that Mr. Gandhi is not leading his followers in the direction of the promised land. He is not only going in the opposite direction but instead of toughening our fibre by a life of toil and struggle is endeavouring to entirely emasculate us and render us altogether unfit for the glorious destiny that, but for him and others like him, is awaiting us.

This will be clear once the nature of his agitation is realised. For that purpose, it is necessary to understand his mentality and his real views on the problems of life and the various questions now in debate.

These are given in various books which have been published and in his paper "Young

India ", edited by him. His " Indian Home Rule ", was first published in 1908. In a publication of 1921, he says " I withdraw nothing except one word of it and that in difference to a lady friend." The reason is the indelicacy of the expression........

The book is in the form of a dialogue between a Reader and the " Editor ", the latter being Gandhi himself.

Mr. Gandhi wishes to know the necessity of driving away the English,

Reader :—" Because India has become impoverished by their Government. They take away our money from year to year. The most important posts are reserved for themselves. We are kept in a state of slavery. They behave insolently towards us, and disregard our feelings."

Gandhi :—" Supposing we get Self-government similar to what the Canadians and South Africans have, will it be good enough ? "

Reader :—" That question also is useless. We may get it when we have the same powers. We shall then hoist our own flag. As is Japan so must India be. We must own our navy, our army, and we must have our own splendour. Then will India's voice ring throughout the world.

Gandhi :—You have well drawn the picture. In effect it means this : that we want English Rule without the Englishman. You want the tiger's nature but not the tiger; that is to say you would make India English and when it becomes English, it will be called not Hindustan but Englistan. *This is not the Swaraj that I want.*

Nothing can be clearer. He does not want the dominion status of Canada or South Africa for India. He does not claim the independence of Japan for India as he points out a few lines below, "What you call swaraj is not truly swaraj."

What is then the real "Swaraj" according to Mr. Gandhi? He proceeds to develope his views by illustrations.

He gives his views on the poverty of India. He says Railways, Lawyers and Doctors have impoverished the country, so much so that, if we do not wake up in time, we shall be ruined.

About railways he says as follows:—

"Man is so made by nature as to require him to restrict his movements as far as his hands and feet will take him. If we did not rush about from place to place by means of railways and such other maddening conveniences, much of the confusion that arises, would be obviated. Our difficulties are of our own creation. God set a limit to a man's locomotive ambition in the construction of his body. Man immediately proceeded to discover means of overriding the limit. God gifted man with intellect that he might know his Maker. Man abused it so that he might forget his Maker. I am so constructed that I can only serve my immediate neighbours, but in my conceit, I pretend to have discovered that I must with my body serve every individual in the Universe. In thus attempting the impossible, man comes in contact with different religionsand is utterly confounded. According to this reasoning, it must be apparent to you that railways are a most dangerous institution. Man has gone further away from his Maker".

And he advises all his friends to go into the interior of the country that has yet not been polluted by the railways and live there in order to be patriotic.

I shall not insult the intelligence of my reader by attempting a defence of the railways which have knit India together. I will only observe that according to Mr. Gandhi, the construction and use of railways for locomotion not possible for man in his natural condition, is an abuse of God's gift. And why? Because if he comes into contact with different natures, with different religions he might try to serve others than his neighbour whom alone God intended him to serve !!!

As to lawyers, he will have none of them; without lawyers, courts could not have been established or conducted and without them the British could not hold India. He has yet to learn that there were courts both in pre-British India and British India before lawyers. He thinks the Hindu-Mahomedan quarrels have often been due to the intervention of lawyers. He wants all people to settle their own quarrels; "men were less unmanly if they settled their disputes either by fighting or by asking their relatives to decide them. They became more unmanly and cowardly when they resorted to the Courts of Law. It is a sign of savagery to settle disputes by fighting. It is not the less so by asking a third party to decide between you and me. The parties alone know who is right and therefore they ought to settle it". Such is his opinion of lawyers and of Courts.

He is even more harsh on doctors. His opinion is quoted below as any statement of it in my own words might be regarded as travesty:—

Let us consider; the business of a doctor is to take care of the body, or, properly speaking, not even that. Their business is really to rid the body of diseases that may afflict. How do these diseasese arise? Surely by our negligence or indulgence. I overeat, I have indigestion, I go to a doctor, he gives me medicine. I am cured, I overeat again, and I take his pills again. Had I not taken the pills in the first instance, I would have suffered the punishment deserved by me, and I would not have over-eaten again. The doctor intervened and helped me to indulge myself. My body thereby certainly felt more at ease, but my mind became weakened. A continuance of a course of medicine must, therefore, result in loss of a control over the mind.

"I have indulged in vice, I contract a disease, a doctor cures me, the odds are that I shall repeat the vice. Had the doctor not intervened, nature would have done its work, and I would have acquired mastery over myself, would have been freed from vice, and would have become happy.

"Hospitals are institutions for propagating sin. Men take less care of their bodies, and immorality increases".

He says therefore that a doctor should "give up medicine, and understand that rather than mending bodies, he should mend souls", and he must also understand that "if, by not taking drugs, perchance the patient dies, the world will not come to grief and he will have been really useful to him".

There is no use in arguing with him and his dupes on this subject after this. But his views must be borne in mind when we come to deal with the present agitation.

About education, his views are equally remarkable. If, he says, education simply means knowledge of letters it is merely an instrument and an instrument may be well used or abused. He adds :—

"We daily observe that many men abuse it and very few make good use of it".

He will not give any education to a raiyat or poor peasant :—

"The ordinary meaning of education is a knowledge of letters. To teach boys reading, writing and arithmetic is called primary education".

"What do you propose to do by giving him a knowledge of letters? Will you add an inch to his happiness? Do you wish to make him discontented with his cottage or his lot?"

So much for primary education. As to higher education he says he has learnt Geography, Astronomy, Algebra, Geometry etc, but neither has that learning benefitted him nor any body about him. As to knowledge of English, it is only useful to enslave people :—

"The foundation that Macaulay laid of education". he says: "has enslaved us. It is worth noting that by receiving English education, we have enslaved the nation. Hypocrisy, tyranny etc. have increased; English-knowing Indians have not hesitated to cheat and strike terror into the people. Now, if we are doing anything for the people at all, we are paying only a portion of the debt due to them".

I shall have to deal with this question of

education later in connection with this appeal to the boys to leave the schools and colleges.

After all this, it will not surprise any one to be told that we must have nothing to do with machinery :—

"It was not that we did not know how to invent machinery, but our forefathers knew that, if we set our hearts after such things, we would become slaves and lose our moral fibre. They, therefore, after due deliberation, decided that we should only do what we could with our hands and feet. They saw that our real happiness and health consisted in a proper use of our hands and feet"

He would not therefore have mills for the reason that machinery is the chief symbol of modern civilisation and it has already begun to desolate Europe. In his opinion it were better for us to send money to Manchester and to use flimsy Manchester cloth than to multiply mills in India. I wonder why he does not ask Lancashire to pay him his crore of rupees. Lancashire would no doubt do so in consideration of the monopoly of supplying India with manufactured goods and India would, according to Mr. Gandhi, get Swaraj. India does not want manufuactured goods ; he asks :—

"What did India do before these articles were introduced? Precisely the same should be done to day. As long as we cannot make pins without machinery, so long will we do without them. The tinsel splendour of glassware we will have nothing to do with, and we will make wick, as of old, with home grown cotton, and use hand-made earthen saucers for Lamps". He finally adds: "I cannot recall a single good point in connectlon with machinery."

Mr. Gandhi wrote his book in 1908 after a visit to England when the Liberal and the Labour parties were carrying on their great campaign in favour of the working men and against the capitalists and Lloyd George was about to launch his great land compaign. He seems to have been impressed with the horrors of the condition of the wage earners which was then portrayed in dark colours in order to support that campaign. His mind, emotional and ill balanced, seems to have been entirely upset by the descriptions that he had then read. He is on the fringe of a large question about which he seems to have been singularly ill informed. In England there is not at this time and there was not when he wrote, any question of the destruction of machinery which is a necessary adjunct to the industrial system.

The questions under debate are the conditions of labour and the distribution of the wealth created by machinery between capitalists and labour. These questions have been under consideration now for some years; the condition of the labourers is being slowly improved, a minimum wage has been introduced and there is a prospect of a still more equitable distribution of the proceeds between capital and labour. Mr. Gandhi says that he has read Dutt's book on the decline of Indian industries but he does not seem to have learnt the lesson inculcated therein—that it is necessary to improve our industries not only to meet the needs of the people of the country, find employment for our labouring population, but also not to force them to compete with the cultivating classes. In India the same problem as in England awaits us. We have to see that the condition of the labourers in the mills and in the other industries is improved. In asking for the ruin of all our manufacturing industries Mr. Gandhi is only playing into the hands of our opponents. He will find strong support in this respect from Lancashire who will, according to some Indian publicists, only be too willing to take any steps to effect the destruction of our competing industries. If he had directed half the energy of his non-co-operation campaign to improving the conditions of the workmen in all our industries he might possibly have succeeded in getting rid of many of those evils which in his opinion require elimination of all machinery and of all industrial undertakings. The other reason for the deplorable condition of the industrial workmen in England is the congestion and overcrowding, in the industrial centres. This is due to a great extent to the action of the landlords who will not allow any expansion of those industrial centres in order to increase the value of their land and thus to exploit the community. In India we have not got that trouble. There is ample room for extension except in Bombay, in all the industrial centres and even in Bombay the difficulty is not due, so far as I am informed to the action of landlords but to natural conditions arising out of the geography of Bombay. Machinery is essential to the creation of wealth by manufacturing industries. The evils that have been portrayed by Mr. Gandhi can be and are being removed by patient effort. His tirade against machinery and mill industries on account of the evils he has witnessed in the West, is due to his ignorance ; a little knowledge in his case has proved a dangerous thing. It is this feeling which has led him to advocate the universal use of spinning wheel in India. This might be useful as a cottage or home industry. It might find work for some who would otherwise be idle. But he is living in a fool's paradise if he considers it a substitute for or will supplant, machinery.

It is unnecessary to say that he hates Parliaments :—

" The condition of England at present is pitiable. I pray to God that India may never be in that plight. That which you consider to be Mother of Parliaments is like a sterile woman and a prostitute. Both these are harsh terms, but exactly fit the case. That Parliament has not yet of its own accord done a single good thing; hence I have compared it to a sterile woman. The natural condition of that Parliament is such that without out-side pressure it can do nothing. It is like a prostitute because it is under the control of ministers who change from time to time. To-day it is under Mr. Asquith ; tomorrow it may be under Mr. Balfour."

" If the money and the time wasted by Parliament were entrusted to a few good men, the English nation would be occupying to-day a much higher platform.

The Parliament is simply a costly toy of the nation. These views are by no means peculiar to me. Some great English thinkers have expressed them.

"That you cannot accept my views at once is only right. 'If you will read the literature on this subject, you will have some idea of it. The Parliament is without a real master, under the Prime Minister, its movement is not steady, but it is buffetted about like a prostitute. The Prime Minister is more concerned about his power than about the welfare of the Parliament. His energy is concentrated upon securing the success of his party. His care is not always that the Parliament shall do right. Prime Ministers are known to have made the Parliament do things merely for party advantage. All this is worth thinking over."

It is no wonder that he called upon all his followers to boycott the Indian Councils. I shall deal with this when dealing with the boycott question.

After all this one would naturally think that if we expel the English from India we would be happy. Not a bit, says Mr. Gandhi whose views about independence are peculiar. Look, he says, at Italy. He thinks that Italy has not gained anything by independence of Austrain domination. He adds :—

"If you believe that because Italians hold Italy, the Italian nation is happy, you are groping in darkness". "What substantial gain did Italy obtain after the withdrawal of the Austrian troops? The gain is only nominal. You do not want therefore to reproduce the same conditions in India. India to gain her independence can fight like Italy only when she has arms and in order to gain her independence India has to be armed and to arm India on a large scale is to Europeanise it. Then her condition will be just as pitiable as that of Europe. This means in short, that India must accept European civilisation ...but the fact is that the Indian nation will not adopt arms and it is well that she does not."

She must not therefore use force to fight the English.

But what is it she has to do. She must obtain Swaraj or Home Rule by 'soul force' What is it?:—

"When we are slaves we think that the whole universe is enslaved. Because we are in an abject condition, we think that the whole of India is in that condition. As a matter of fact, it is not so, but it is as well to impute our slavery to the whole of India. But if we bear in mind the above fact we can see that if we become free, India is free. And in this thought you have definition of 'swaraj.' It is 'swaraj' when we earn to rule ourselves. It is therefore in the palm of our hands. Do not consider this 'swaraj' to be like a dream. Hence there is no idea of sitting still. The 'swaraj' that I wish to picture before you and me is such that, after we have once realised it, we will endeavour to the end of our lifetime to persuade others to do likewise. But such 'swaraj' has to be experienced by each one for himself."

The assumption made by a few persons that Mr. Gandhi is only condemning parliamentary government for its inutility is unfounded. The extracts already given might lend some colour to that view. But such is not the fact. In England Parliamentary government is denounced by certain persons on the ground that it will always be under the influence of a capitalist Press and therefore unable to redress the evils from which the people of the country other than the capitalists are suffering. Mr. Gandhi's objection is not based on any such ground; he is against not only Parliamentary Government but practically against any Government in any form as is apparent from the extracts given above. The doctrine that Governments have very little to do with our happiness which depends upon self-control or 'soul force' has many advocates, but to deduce it as a doctrine from the alleged failure of Parliamentary Government in England is ludicrous. I shall not stop here to justify Parliamentary government which has justified itself by its results; it is only ignorance of the work that has been done which is responsible for opinions like those to which Mr. Gandhi has given expression.

Towards the end of the book he says :—

Before I leave you, I will take the liberty of repeating :—

1. Real Home Rule is Self Rule or control

2. The way to it is Passive Resistance; that is soul force or love force;

In my opinion, we have used the term "Swaraj" without understanding its real significance. I have endeavoured to explain it as I understand it, and my conscience testifies that *my life henceforth is dedicated to its attainment.*

Such is the real Gandhi. Railways, lawyers, courts, doctors, education on Western lines, machinery of every kind or manufacturing industries, parliamentary government should disappear. He is singularly ill informed on every one of the questions he has discussed. 'Soul force' alone should be relied upon. No resistance should be offered to violence. No resistance should be offered to robbery and the robbers are to be left to cut one another's throats. No resistance to be offered to murderers or to those who might want to enslave you. Briefly, no protection is to be given by laws and their administrators to person and property.

There is no harm perhaps as long as such fantastic visionaries restrict the application of these principles to themselves, to their own persons or properties. But it becomes a serious matter when their general application is sought for.

These are the sentiments he expressed in 1908, and it was with these sentiments that he came to India. As it is well to be definite and clear, I will quote from a letter addressed by him in 1909 to a friend in India :—

"Bombay, Calcutta and the other chief cities of India are the real plague spots".

"If British rule were replaced tomorrow by Indian rule based on modern methods, India would be no better, except that she would be able then to retain some of the money that is drained away to England; but then India would only become a second or fifth nation of Europe or America".

"Medical science is the concentrated essence of black magic. Quackery is infinitely preferable to what passes for high medical skill".

"Hospitals are the instruments that the devil has been using for his own purpose, in order to keep his hold on his kingdom. They perpetuate vice, misery and degradation and real slavery".

"India's salvation consists in unlearning what she has learnt during the past fifty years. The railways, telegraphs, hospitals, lawyers, doctors, and such like have all to go, and so called upper classes have to learn to live consciously and religiously and deliberately the simple peasant life, knowing it to be a life giving true happiness".

But he soon found that it was hopeless to carry out his theories in the face of the determination of the people of India to attain Home Rule preached by the Indian National Congress and the Indian politicians. He had accordingly to put on a new garb. Therefore, in 1917, the year of the famous declaration made by the British Government about the progressive realisation of self government, he found it necessary, to obtain a hearing, to accept the Home Rule programme. In his Presidential address at the First Gujarat Political Conference in 1917 he said that without going into the merits of the scheme of reforms approved by the Congress and the Muslim League he will do all that is necessary to get it accepted and enforced. Though the scheme itself is not 'swaraj, he admitted it was a great step towards 'swaraj'. At the same time he said that though he is acting on the propriety of the current trend of thought it does not appear to him to be tending altogether in the right direction as the 'swaraj' put forward is one of Western type. Nevertheless as India is being governed in accordance with the Western system and without Parliament we should be nowhere, he does not hesitate to take part in the Parliamentary swaraj movement and the programme that he sketched out for himself may be described thus in his own words written in 1921 :—

"But I would warn the reader against thinking that I am to-day aiming at the Swaraj therein (spritual swaraj as described in his 'Indian Home Rule'), I know that India is not ripe for it. It may seem an impertinence to say so. But such is my conviction. I am individually working for the self-rule pictured therein. But to-day my corporate activity is undoubtedly devoted to the attainment of Parliamentary Swaraj in accordance with the wishes of the people of India. I am not aiming at destroying railways or hospitals, though I would certainly welcome their natural destruction. Neither railways nor hospitals are a test of a high and pure civilisation. At best they are a necessary evil. Neither adds one inch to the moral stature of a nation. Nor am I aiming at a permanent destruction of law courts, much as I regard it as 'a consummation devoutly to be wished for,' still less am I trying to destroy all machinery and mills. It requires a higher simplicity and renunciation than the people are to-day prepared for"

He also admitted that his acceptance of Parliamentary Swaraj required some modification of his theory of using violence or force. He admitted that though there is no scope for violence or force in spiritual swaraj, and military training is intended only for those who do not believe in it, he was prepared to accept the view that the whole of India will never accept Satyagraha. He added :—

'Not to defend the weak is an entirely effeminate idea, everywhere to be rejected. In order to protect our innocent sister from the brutal designs of a man we ought to offer ourselves a willing sacrifice and by the force of Love conquer the brute in the man. But if we have not attained that power, we would certainly use up all our bodily strength in order to frustrate those designs. The votaries of soul force and brute force are both soldiers. The latter, bereft of his arms, acknowledges defeat, the former does not know what defeat is".

It was a consequence of this acceptance of Parliamentary Swaraj that he should try to work the Montagu Chelmsford Council reforms. Though these reforms may be inadequate yet for one who accepts the goal of Parliamentary Government it was his bounden duty to avail himself of the available Parliamentary scheme to carry out those reforms which were then possible and to take the necessary steps to enlarge the scope of the scheme to carry out the further reforms that might be needed. Accordingly at the Amritsar Congress in December 1919, he resolved to co-operate with the country in working the Reform Scheme.

I have already pointed out that he entirely disagreed with the system of Parliamentary government and his acceptance was one of necessity. At the earliest opportunity at the special sessions of the Indian National Congress held at Calcutta in September 1920 and at the National Congress held at Nagpur in December 1920 he took steps to destroy the Montagu Reform Scheme of Parliamentary Swaraj and everything else to which he had given a reluctant assent and to bring the country to adopt his wild theories already stated by me and in order to do so, he brought into prominence forces entirely opposed to his own principles which he proved himself unable to control with disastrous consequences and had to resort willingly or unwillingly to dishonest methods.

What was the reason for his throwing over overboard the Montagu Reform Scheme? The following resolution which at his instance was passed by the National Congress at Calcutta and practically re-affirmed at Nagpur will explain the situation as then developed.

THE NON-CO-OPERATION RESOLUTION

"In view of the fact that on the Khilafat question both the Indian and Imperial Governments have signally failed in their duty towards the Musalmans of India, and the Prime Minister has deliberately broken his pledged word given to them, and that it is the duty of every non-Moslem Indian in every legitimate manner to assist his Musalman brother in his attempt to remove the religious calamity that has over taken him :—

"And in view of the fact that in the matter of the events of the April 1919 both the said Governments have grossly neglected or failed to protect the innocent people of the Punjab and punish officers guilty of unsoldierly and barbarous behaviour towards them and have exonerated Sir Michael O'Dwyer who proved himself directly or indirectly responsible for the most official crimes and callous to the sufferings of the people placed under his administration, and that the debate in the House of Lords betrayed a woeful lack of sympathy with the people of India and showed virtual support of the systematic terrorism and frightfulness adopted in the Punjab and that the latest Viceregal pronouncement is proof of entire absence of repentance in the matters of the Khilafat and the Punjab.

"This Congress is of opinion that there can be no contentment in India without redress of the two afore-mentioned wrongs, and that the only effectual means to vindicate national honour and to prevent a repetition of similar wrongs in future is the establishment of Swarajya. This Congress is further of opinion that there is no course left open for the people of India but to approve of and adopt the policy of progressive non-violent non-co-operation until the said wrongs are righted and Swarajya is established.

"And inasmuch as a beginning should be made by the classes who have hitherto moulded and represented opinion and inasmuch as Government consolidates its power through titles and honours bestowed on the people, through schools controlled by it, its law courts and its legislative councils, and inasmuch as it is desirable in the prosecution of the movement to take the minimum risk and to call for the least sacrifice compatible with the attainment of the desired object, this Congress earnestly advises.:—

(*a*) surrender of titles and honorary offices and resignation from nominated seats in local bodies;

(*b*) refusal to attend Government Levees, Durbars and other official and semi-official functions held by Government officials or in their honour;

(*c*) gradual withdrawal of children from Schools and colleges owned, aided or controlled by Government and in place of such schools and colleges in the establishment of National Schools and Colleges in the various Provinces;

(*d*) gradual boycott of British Courts by lawyers and litigants and establishment of private arbitration courts by their aid for the settlement of private disputes;

(*e*) refusal on the part of the military, clerical and labouring classes to offer themselves as recruits for service in Mesopotamia;

(*f*) withdrawal by canditates of their candidature for election to the Reformed Councils and refusal on the part of the voters for any candidate who may despite the Congress advice offer himself for election; and

(*g*) the boycott of foreign goods.

"And inasmuch as non-co-operation has been conceived of as a measure of discipline and self-sacrifice without which no nation can make real progress, and inasmuch as an opportunity should be given in the very first stage of non-co-operation to every man, woman and child, for such discipline and self-sacrifice, this Congress advices adoption of Swadeshi in piecegoods on a vast scale, and inasmuch as the existing mills of India with indigenous capital and control do not manufacture sufficient yarn and sufficient cloth for the requirements of the nation, and are not likely to do so for a long time to come this Congress advises immediate stimulation of further manufacture on a large scale by means of reviving hand-spinning in every home and hand weaving on the part of the millions of weavers who have abandoned their ancient and honourable calling for want of encouragement.

The Khilafat question first, the Punjab wrongs next are given as the two grounds for discarding the Reform Scheme and demanding Swarajya or immediate Home Rule for the prevention of similar wrongs in future. For the attainment of such Swarajya or immediate Home Rule a policy of what is called non-violent non-co-operation is advocated and as a beginning the people are advised to take certain steps which are therein referred to. Though discarding the Montagu Chelmsford Reform Scheme of Home Rule by certain stages, Mr. Gandhi says he is working for immediate Home Rule in accordance with the Resolution, to me it seems clear what he is really aiming at is not Home Rule of any kind or form *i. e.* Parliamentary Government with absolute powers, but Swarajya or Home Rule, as he himself has outlined it in his Indian Home Rule, the purport of which I have briefly given above. *i. e.* anarchy and soul force. I shall now attempt to show that there were no adequate reasons to discard the Reform Scheme of Home Rule for a scheme of immediate Home Rule and that the steps proposed to be taken are not calculated to attain Home Rule of any kind or form but are steps intended for Gandhi Swarajya which means anarchy or soul force.

In considering these questions the object of this movement must not be lost sight of. In Mr. Gandhi's own words "Non-co-peration though a religious and strictly moral movement deliberately aims at the overthrow of the Government." Prima facie therefore all steps taken in pursuance of this resolution are intended for this purpose.

I propose first of all to take up the Khilafat question which stands first in the Resolution.

THE KHILAFAT QUESTION

With reference to this Khilafat agitation it is important to bear this in mind. After the armistice of 1918, there were two memorials presented on behalf of Turkey by the Muslim residents in England, one in January 1919 soon after the armistice, which included the names of His Highness the Aga Khan, Abbas Ali Baig, Rt. Hon. Ameer Ali, Messrs : Yusaf Ali, H. K. Kidwai etc.; and one at the end of the year in December 1919, the signatories therof included such Mahomedans as the following: H. H. Aga Khan, Rt. Hon. Ameer Ali, Hon. Mr. Bhurgi, Mr. M. H. Kidwai. Both included many non-mahomedans, some of them of great-influence and position. They claimed for Turkey, Constantinople, Thrace, Anatolia including Smyrna. There was no claim for the countries occupied by those who were not Turks.

The Indian Mahomedan claim went much

further. By the deputation to the Viceroy towards the end of that year and by the subsequent deputation to the Prime Minister and others the claim was advanced for the restoration of Turkey to the pre-war state, giving Home Rule if necessary to the Armenians or the Arabs etc. under Turkish sovereignty. This of course was an impossible demand. The Arabs are entitled to as much consideration as the Turks. Mahomad Ali and Shaukat Ali are really responsible for this claim.

Another claim advocated in the Council of State in India was to let Turkey have Anatolia and Thrace ; full independence be given to the Arabs and the countries inhabited by them without any control by any non-muslim power. Whether the evacuation of Aden is included in this, I am unable to say.

The Indian Mahomedan agitation has become a danger to the State on account of the failure of the Secretary of State and Government of India to tell the Indian Mahomedans that they, the Government have nothing to do with the Khilafat question ; that their responsibility is confined to representing to the British cabinet the feelings of the Indian Mahomedans, and the ultimate decision will depend upon what is good for the Empire as a whole.

But so far as Gandhi was concerned the position is quite clear. He puts forward whichever is the most extreme demand made by the Khilafat party without any enquiry as to their reasonableness. He relies upon a 'promise' made by Lloyd George in favour of Turkey about their home lands and Thrace discarding at the same time the limitation contained in the promise to the subject races that they will not again be placed under Turkey. He relies upon another statement made by Lloyd George that after this, recruitment went up. The fact is that the recruitment of non Mahomedans also went up and both were due to Sir Michal O'Dwyer. Though he now denies having insisted upon the evacuation of Egypt by England as a necessary condition of satisfaction of the Khilafat claim, he insists upon the withdrawal of the Indian troops. For what purpose he does not explain nor does he say whether he wants England to evacaute Egypt. He knows, I presume, that Egypt has repudiated the Caliph's authority. He was not apparently aware that the Arabs will not recognize the supremacy of any Turkish power. But this is no difficulty to him. For if that turns out to be the case he says the Arab Chief who held sway over Mecca and Medina might become the Khalif. That Syria is not under England did not matter. He wants the non-co-operators to be satisfied by England that she was not in any way responsible for the French occupation or retention of Syria, in which case he is willing to excuse her. He fails to appreciate the weight of what appears to be an insuperable objection that the Turks and their Khalif do not want any domination over Arabia but, as they said in their deputation in January-February, 1919, after the armistice, only wanted to be left alone with economic and political independence in their own ethnological area. Neither Mr. Gandhi nor the Khilafat advocates show any realisation of this fact. With a light heart they maintain that the question is not Turkish but Mahomedan and therefore Turkish opinion alone cannot decide the question. Palestine, of course, according to Mr. Gandhi, must be under Turkish sovereignty. It is enough for him that the prophet of Arabia has so willed it. The prophets of

Israel or the founder of Christianity, Jewish or Christian sentiments, are as nothing in the balance. The real truth of course is that in the case of the Khilafat agitation Mr. Gandhi and some of its most active and prominent leaders want to use the agitation to destroy the Government and not to effect a real settlement of the question. The most energetic of the promoters of the movement were Mohomed Ali and Shaukat Ali. They were active members of the Muslim League advocating Mahomedan interests in opposition to the Hindus in the old days of the Bengal Partition agitation. In their public speeches they emphasised the identity of the interests of the Indian Mahomedans with the interests of the Mahomedans elsewhere in Tripoli and Algeria in preference to those of the Hindus, though living under the same Government with them. Since the Balkan wars, however, on account of their intense hatred towards the British Government for their failure to assist their co-religionists in the West, they found it politic to approach the Hindus. Then followed the internment of the brothers which naturally still more embittered their feelings towards the Government.

During the internment they did not cease to preach sermons of virulence against the Government, and even after their release they did not cease their propaganda of hatred against the British Government. The independence of India—no doubt as a preliminary step towards a subsequent Mahomedan domination in India—was as much their object as the full restoration of the Khilafat domination to its pre-war condition. This was avowed by the Ali Brothers themselves. Mr. Shaukat Ali said in April 1920:—

> "We do not embark on this step without fully realising what it means. It means a movement for absolute independence."

In fact, to those who know them or who have read the proceedings of their trial no evidence of this kind is required.

At the Khilafat Conference in Karachi—of which they were the guiding spirits—held on the 9th of July 1921 the following resolution calling upon the Mohomedan sepoys to desert in the name of religion was passed;

> "The meeting clearly proclaims that it is in every way religiously unlawful for a Mussalman at the present movement to continue in the British Army or to induce others to join the army, and it is the duty of all the

Mussalmans in general and Ulemas in particular to see that these religious commandments are brought home to every Mussalman in the army and that if no settlement is arrived at before Christmas regarding our campaign an Indian republic will be declared at the Ahmedabad sessions of the Congress."

The two brothers were tried and convicted by the ordinary civil courts, and the judge pointed out that however lawful and constitutional the Khilafat committee may have been in its origin, however permissible the agitation carried on in its earlier stages, those who were controlling it soon began to rely on dangerous religious propaganda. About them he said: "They had seen them in Court, heard their statements in the Lower Court and their speeches here, and they could have no doubt that with the exception of accused No. Six (a Hindu) they openly gloried in their hatred of the Government of India and the British name. They justified the above resolution by the religious law of the Koran which they said the Mussalmans are bound to follow even when opposed to the law of the land. All the Mohamedans in this case including Mohamad Ali and Shaukat Ali maintained, "first, that their religion compels them to do certain acts, secondly, that no law which restrains them from doing those acts which their religion compels them to do has any validity, and thirdly, that in answer to a charge of breaking the law of the land it is sufficient to raise and prove the plea that the act which is alleged to be an offence is one which is enjoyed by their religion."

It is impossible to believe that Gandhi and his adherents are not aware that this claim of the Mahomedans to be judged only by the law of the Koran, is a claim which is the *fons et origo* of all Khilafat claims of whatever kind. It is as well to be clear about this, for not only does the acceptance of the claim mean the death knell of the British Empire or Indo-British commonwealth, whatever name we may care to give to the great fraternity of nations to which we belong, but specifically as regards India it means a real denial of Swaraj. For it involves Mahomedan rule and Hindu subjection or Hindu Rule and Mahomedan subjection. Let there be no mistake about this, no camouflage. Whatever the Hindus may mean by the Hindu Muslim entente, and I believe they mean a true equality, and whatever the more enlightened Mussalmans may mean, Mohamad Ali, Shaukat Ali, and those of their persuasion, mean a Mussalman dominion pure and simple, though they are of course clever enough to keep the cat in the bag so long as the time for its emergence is yet unripe. They protest, it need hardly be said, that they are animated by no *arricre pensee*, no sectarian spirit, only by the most loving goodwill towards the Hindu brethren. But there are some of us who are too experienced to be caught by this mischievous and pernicious chaff and must sound the warning to those less experienced and more gullible. Considering the high character of some of the men who follow Gandhi, I can only believe that this realization came to them so late that it was difficult for them to withdraw.

As pointed out in the Karachi trial, these movements at first appear innocuous, then grow dangerous.

The Khilafat associations throughout the country were intended to carry on the "non-violent non-co-operation" campaign against Government. The process of evolution from ostensible non-violence at first to violence is so well described by Mr. Macpherson speaking in the Legislative Council that I have quoted it (App. XVI). It applies to all organisations, but with greater force to Khilafat for reasons arising out of Islam which will be shortly explained. There is no judicial description of this development in Malabar, the most notorious instance. I shall content myself, therefore, with giving a summary of the judgment convicting certain persons for a riot in Malegaon in April, 1920. So early had lawlessness in this form begun to show itself. It will also explain the methods adopted.

A political movement began in Malegaon on the 15th March 1920, when a "Khilafat Committee" and a body of "volunteers" were formed. The Committee's activities took the shape of lectures and "wazas". The lectures were political and the "wazas" are said to have been religious sermons. In January, 1921, Shaukat Ali visited the town and lectured on the Khilafat movement. It was shortly after this visit that political activity became intensified.

The two Mahomedan schools, the Beitu-lullum and the Anjuman school, used to receive grants-in-aid from Government. Money was raised to enable the two State-aided schools to refuse the Government grant-in-aid in pursuance of the non-co-operation movement, and a few Hindus were members of the party. The collections were to be made by means of a "paisa" fund, an old idea. Every person selling a "sari", that is all the weavers in Malegaon, were required to pay a "paisa" or quarter of an anna to the fund.

The system left practically no option to the weavers who objected to pay the "paisa". Objecting buyers were encountered by persecution. The fund Committee called a public meeting on the 27th February, at which it was resolved that the buyers refusing to make the collections as directed should be commercially boycotted. The commercial boycott of the recalcitrant buyers was enforced by picketting their shops with volunteers and their business was stopped. The former had appealed for protection to the authorities by applications and petitions, but so long as nothing actually illegal was done these were powerless actively to interfere.

Meanwhile lectures and "wazas" were being

continually held in the open spaces in the town and excitement was running high. On the reports made to him the District Magistrate came to the conclusion that in a place like Malegaon which is ill-lighted the carrying of swords and cudgels at public meetings at night by volunteers was likely to lead to a breach of the peace. He therefore issued a proclamation on the 30th March prohibiting the practice. It was a breach of the terms of this proclamation and its enforcement by prosecutions which was the immediate excuse for the riot.

But the local authorities had also tried to allay the friction and excitement in other ways. The Sub-Divisional Officer, had called a meeting on the 13th March with a view to find a method of collection of the Fund which might put an end to the trouble about it and stop enforced contributions. Collection boxes were recommended, but nothing definite was agreed to by the other side.

Some of the leaders were persuaded to issue a manifesto which was signed by eleven persons. This manifesto quotes Mr. Gandhi's dictates to non-violence and exhorts the volunteers not to carry cudgels and recommends that only peaceful methods should be used in collecting the Funds.

It clearly had little effect. One of the men who signed it, on the 4th April (it had been issued on the 1st April) at a public meeting apologized for it on his own and the other signatories' behalf and they were pardoned for having signed it. Meanwhile the boycotting and picketting of the shops of the Anti-Fund people was continued. On the 15th prosecutions were instituted against 24 volunteers for a breach of the District Magistrate's proclamation of the 30th March. On the 24th April, the day before the hearing of these cases, a meeting was again called at night at which a leading Mahomedan is reported to have used the following words :—

"They must not be afraid of Government or of the police and that the volunteers would see about the cases brought against them and may God give the volunteers strength to promote their religion." The next day April 25th twelve of these cases came on for hearing before Mr. Thakar the Resident Magistrate. They ended in the conviction of the 6 volunteers and their being fined Rs. 50 each with the alternative of 4 weeks' simple imprisonment. The fines were not paid.

On the result being known the mob that had collected gave vent to their feelings by loud cries of "Alla-ho-akbar," the war cry used by the mob throughout the riot, assaulted all the police to be found in the town of Malegoan, burned a temple, killed the Sub-Inspector of Police, not the only one killed and threw his body into the fire and looted the houses of all who were opposed to the Khilafat movement, the owners themselves having fled in the meantime.

This illustrates the 'non-violent' methods followed by the khilafat committees and volunteers. I give another instance in full for illustration Barabanki (App. XI) which shows perhaps more forcibly the violent fanaticism supporting the movement. More instances can be easily given.

The development from an apparently peaceful to a revolutionary attitude is strikingly illustrated in the Khilafat agitation not only by revolutionary activities but by open declaration. The resolution of the Karachi Conference showed the Mahomedan intention to declare independence and proclaim an Indian Republic at the following Congress at Ahmedabad in December 1921. A resolution for absolute independence was actually passed in the Subjects Committee of the Khilafat Conference at Ahmedabad, but was not passed at the Conference itself only because the President ruled it out of order. But immediately after the meeting formally closed, the motion was passed by the members of the Conference at the instance of the President of Muslim League whose speech as President will amply repay perusal (App. XVIII). He was in effect only carrying out at the Khilafat Conference the intention of the Karachi Conference of which the Ali Brothers were the moving spirits. In his speech he points out, what in effect is apparent to all, that Islam is opposed to non-violence and, as he said in the course of one of his speeches, the Mussalmans accepted it on the promise of Mr. Gandhi to secure Swaraj within a year. It was a legitimate move therefore to proclaim a rebellion. Another difference in principle was pointed out which is productive of frightful consequences and must alienate Hindus from Mahomedans. The Ali Brothers had already said that if the Afghans invaded India to wage a holy war the Indian Mahomedans are not only bound to fight them but also to fight the Hindus if they refuse to co-operate with them. When therefore Gandhi and his followers fraternised with the Khilafatists, the latter had no doubt of their support if eventually it came to rebellion. They were confirmed in this by Gandhi's attitude on the questions in issue between them and the Hindus. He advises the latter Hindus—to submit themselves to Mahomedan dictation. He begs them not to insist on the prohibition of the cow slaughter by Mahomedans and to rely upon Mahomedan forbearance to afford them relief in that direction. On the other hand he advises the Hindus to refrain from irritating the Mahomedans by insisting on carrying their processions past the mosques on their religious occasions. He advises them to study Hindustani as against Hindi; in fact complete submission to the Muslim feelings in all matters in controversy between them. His attitude towards the Mopla outrages shows the extent of his surrender. His alliance with the

Khilafat movement has led to frightful results in Malabar. Relying on the assurance of Gandhi and his followers, of Hindu support for the Khilafat movement, and supported by the teaching that the Hindus may be treated as foes on failure to support them in a holy war, the Moplas when they rose against the British Government were furious at the Hindu attitude of loyalty to England. The result was, themselves, armed and organised they took the Hindus unawares and committed atrocities too well known, to need recapitulation here—butchered them and inflicted injuries on them far worse than death.

For sheer brutality on women, I do not remember anything in history to match the Malabar rebellion. It broke out about the 20th of August. Even by the 6th of September the results were dreadful. The Viceroy's speech made on that date deserves careful attention (App. I)

The atrocities committed more particularly on women are so horrible and unmentionable that I do not propose to refer to them in this book. I have selected a few accounts out of literally hundreds that might be selected from the English and vernacular papers. (App. III.) One narrative is by Mrs. Besant. The resolution passed at a meeting presided over by the Zamorin Maharaja at which, many of the leading Hindus in the District were present enters a strong protest against the attempts made by interested persons to minimize the gravity of the occurrence (App. V.) The moving appeal signed by many ladies headed by the senior Rani of Nilambur who belongs to one of the wealthiest families and were rulers in ancient days shows the nature of the atrocities and the apprehensions still entertained after the rebellion is quelled (App. IV.) I do not think it advisable to publish any more but I would point out in addition to those mentioned in these articles two other forms of torture credibly reported as having been resorted to in the case of men—flaying alive, and making them dig their own graves before their slaughter. It is now ascertained that the Mahomedan's had held frequent meetings in their mosques and, had made all preparations for a rising. Hence it was difficult for the Hindus in these tracts to make any defence or escape. The horrid tragedy continued for months.

Thousands of Mahomedans killed, and wounded by troops, thousands of Hindus butchered, women subjected to shameful indignities, thousands forcibly converted, persons flayed alive, entire families burnt alive, women it is said hundreds throwing themselves into wells to avoid dishonour, violence and terrorism threatening death standing in the way of reversion to their own religion. This is what Malabar in particular owes to the Khilafat agitation, to Gandhi and his Hindu friends. The President of the Indian Moslem League, following the Ali injunction, justified the Mahomedan atrocities as an act of war against the Hindus and the Government. Gandhi too pleaded for the Mahomedans. All this was too much even for their dupes who have entered a spirited protest (App. III). It is impossible after all I have said above that there can be any sympathy with the Khilafat agitation. The future may be envisaged. Gandhi and his dupes have led Khilafatists to understand that the Hindus will stand by them in any contingency, impliedly assuring them, as they believed in Malabar, of support even in resistance to British rule. This Islamic consciousness which looks to a brotherhood beyond India and beyond the Empire does not support the claim for early concession of Home Rule, for Home Rule means Home Rule within the Empire, not outside it—the Home Rule enjoyed by the self-governing constituents of the commonwealth. The Empire, it will be reasonably urged, cannot afford to place great power in the hands of a party which would subordinate the interests of the Empire and of India to the interests of a large body outside the Empire who actually stand in opposition to it. The introduction of this religious element in this manner is fatal to the well-being of the Empire, and unless some other basis can be found for the Hindu-Mahomedan entente, it must go. The extent to which Mr. Gandhi is prepared to go in support of the Khilafat claim is stated in this extract :—

"What will the Imperial Government do if France were to attempt to deprive England of Dover and India were secretly to help France or openly to show indifference or hostility to England's struggle to retain Dover? Can Indians be expected to sit idle when the Khilafat is vivisected?"

It is one thing to ask the Empire or India to go to war in favour of an oppressed class-but to ask her to do it in the interests of co-religionists of a community living outside the Empire is very different.

What is the present position? I shall describe it in the words of one of Mr. Gandhi's dupes, a secretary of a District Congress Committee, Mr. K. Madhavan Nair of Calicut, who writes on January 4th as follows :—

> Now the position is this :—
>
> The Hindus and Mohamedans have been waging a common war with non-violence as the fundamental creed. It has to be noted however, that there is a party led by the Maulana that advocates violence for the achievement of their object. Suppose to-morrow that party takes to violence and the other remains non-violent, what will be the fate of the non-violent party if Maulana's views are pushed to their logical conclusion? Is freedom worth having if in the attainment of it you have to loot, murder and outrage your innocent neighbour who does not agree with you or approve of your methods and is Swaraj possible of achievement and the Khilafat likely to be righted by such means? Maulana's views make. hose who have absolutely no faith in violence to think over these facts deeply and anxiously.

The Indian Non-Mahomedans, did not trouble themselves about the Khilafat claims. Mr. Gandhi and his followers took it up as an anti-British movement to secure Mahomedan support to his non-co-operation movement. Even that non-Mahomedan sympathy with the Khilafat movement, has vanished. That movement acquired its strength on account of such unfortunate statements that the Secretary of State and the Government of India are in hearty sympathy with the Moslim demands; statements like those reported to have been made by His Highness Aga Khan that Mr. Montagu is doing as much as it is possible to support the Mahomedan claim and Gandhi himself could not have done more. I doubt whether any influential newspaper or any publicist in America, England or the continent support the Khilafat claim as advanced by Indian Mahomedans or by Gandhi. However, the reputed sentiments of Mr. Montagu and the Government of India have influenced even moderate Mahomedans and Hindus to support them against the cabinet in starting and supporting an agitation, which has now assumed dangerous proportions.

The Khilafat movement does not want, and Mr. Gandhi is not for, any reasonable settlement of the Mahomedan grievance or for Home Rule. They wish to get rid of the

British Government. Such being the objective naturally the Khilafat Indian agitators have put foward demands which the Turks themselves recognise as outside practical politics. They have hampered the efforts of their friends for a revision of the treaty of Sevres. Everybody now realises that this attitude of the Khilafat movement under the guidance of Gandhi and Mahomed Ali stood in the way of any reasonable settlement. It is a futile endeavour of the Indian and British Governments to satisfy Mr. Gandhi or the Khilafat agitators led by the Ali brothers. Gandhi and his followers have greatly encouraged the growth of Indian Pan Islamism which will in future be always opposed to other Religions and civilizations. I can well understand the adherent of large numbers of Mussulmans to the idea of Pan-Islamism. It must naturally have a fascination for devotees of Islam by reason of the splendour of its promise that Mussulmans the world over shall one day be united under one flag, but we have to take the world as it is and to take into the consideration the forces actually at work in reconstruction. The world has passed the stage of religious empires. It has gone beyond the stage of religious crusades. We are on the threshold of an era of a brotherhood transcending religious differences, transcending even national differences and of which one of the dominant notes is a unity of purpose in which religious differences of race and customs are to be merged and harmonised. Pan-Islamism or Pan-Christianity or Pan-Budhism—one can hardly speak of Pan-Hinduism —belong to the world that is dead and not to the world that is living. They mean destruction, proselytisation, the assertion of superiority the world war was waged to destroy. This also shows the dangerous foundation on which the Gandhi movement rests. Home Rule or Swaraj is claimed not as an end in itself but for the purpose of righting the alleged wrongs sustained by foreigners. We know Gandhi's principles which I have set forth above. Swaraj or political independence is not what he really wants. It is not the Caliph grievances that have led him to claim political independence. He wants to destroy the British Government, as a hater of all Governments.

The attitude of the Government towards the people of the Punjab and the Punjab officials is stated in the Congress Resolution as the second and the only other reason for this non-co-operation compaign against the Government.

THE PUNJAB ATROCITIES

No one feels for the Punjab more than I do. I doubt whether anybody was in a position to know more of it than I was. Even now with all the enquiries made by the Hunter Commission and by the Congress Sub-Committee many deplorable incidents as bad as any, worse perhaps, than any reported have not been disclosed. At this distance of time it is best that they should remain so. It is with a full knowledge of this that I make the following remarks.

The conditions now have entirely changed. Before the Reforms under a Lieutenant-Governor, a single individual, the atrocities in the Punjab which we know only too well, could be committed almost with impunity. Now instead of one man the Government of the Punjab consist not only of a Governor who no doubt is an Englishman, but of an Executive Council consisting of an Englishman and an

Indian, who was a non official before appointment to his seat in the Council and for all practical purposes two Indian Ministers who are also consulted in all important matters. Though, therefore, a repetition of the old incidents may be possible, it is unlikely. The Government of India again, which then consisted of only one Indian, now includes three Indian members, a powerful contingent. Above all, it will be remembered that it was necessary to pass an Act of Indemnity to save the delinquents from proceedings in civil and criminal Courts. Such an Act of Indemnity would scarcely be possible now, with a Legislative Assembly consisting of a majority of elected members under the new constitution, The trouble in the Punjab arose out of the Rowlat Act which is repealed. Many high handed proceedings were taken under the Regulations of 1818 the provisions of which were applied for purposes for which they were never intended. The regulations are now repealed so far as the matters are concerned. Many of these proceedings were taken under the Defence of India Act and they also have gone so that for the future at any rate our position is very different from what it was in the past. In such circumstances what is it that one would expect? If it is an honest endeavour that is being made to solve the difficulties which arose out of the Punjab, one would expect a demand for any further guarantees that may be necessary against a repetition of such occurrences and the punishment of those who have acted not under an error of judgment and not in good faith. But the demands now made are of a very different kind. They do not seek for further guarantees, at least none are formulated.

I realise that the eulogium passed by the English Cabinet on Lord Chemsford and Sir Michael O'Dwyer was an outrage on Indian public opinion. I believe also that the Government of India committed a great political blunder in not publishing their proceedings, punishing the subordinate officials in accordance with the orders of the Cabinet. I agree further that it was an egregious mistake to pass the Indemnity Act when India was so excited. The Government should have waited for the result of the proceedings in Civil or Criminal Courts, when they might have pardoned those who acted in good faith reimbursing their expenses. But that is not the question now. Mr. Gandhi and his party want certain persons to be punished on the strength of the report submitted by the Congress Committee who made an *exparte* enquiry of their own without hearing the other side. This is not right. Moreover every where it is recognised that the security of the subject, person and property, requires that the punishment of the guilty should be in the hands of the Courts and not within the discretion of an Executive Council. If these officers whose punishment is called for are guilty it is the Courts that ought to punish them, and I speak with knowledge when I say that no steps open to them have yet been taken by those who carry on the agitation to vindicate justice. Is it possible, then, to maintain that the Punjab question in any way justifies the tremendous agitation that is being carried on for the dismemberment of the Empire. Besides how is it possible for any reasonable man to say that this affords any justification for not utilizing the Legislative Councils to help the Punjab and to carry out the reforms of which the country is urgently in need. Besides it must be remembered that some of the Punjab political leaders have failed in their duty. During the crisis they refused to come forward to substantiate their complaints of maladministration of Martial Law, even of those matters within their personal knowledge. They did not give a chance to the Government of India to control the Government of the Punjab or the administration of Martial law. *The real truth, of course, is that the Punjab grievances are only a pretext for this agitation, by the violent section headed by Mr. Gandhi. It is really not the redress of the Punjab grievances or prevention of the repetition of atrocities that is sought for, so much as the expulsion of the British Government from India.*

SWARAJ OR HOME RULE

The Resolution says that on account of the failure of Government to redress these grievances we must have 'Swaraj.' It is important to remember that long before these occurrences Mr. Gandhi had come to the conclusion that we must have Independence. It would accordingly seem dishonest on his part to say that these events led him to the demand for Swaraj or Home Rule.

In his scheme of "Home Rule for India" Mr. Gandhi said :—

"Now you will have seen that it is not necessary for us to have as our goal the expulsion of the English. If the English became Indianised we can accommodate them. If they wish to remain in India along with their civilisation, there is no room for them. It lies with us to bring about such a state of things."

Then in reply to the question that it is impossible that Englishmen should ever become Indianised, he says :—

'To say that is equivalent to saying that the English

have no humanity in them. And it is really beside the point whether they become so or not. If we keep our own house in order only those who are fit to live in it will remain. Others will leave of their own accord."

It is something that he gives a loophole to the Englishman to remain in India. To the question that there may be chaos and anarchy on account of the Hindu Mahomedan position he states :—

"I would prefer any day anarchy and chaos in India to an armed peace brought about by the bayonet between the Hindus and Musalmans."

When it was pointed out to him that the dissensions amongst the Hindus themselves may cause the same result he is not dismayed. He says :—

"We are not to assume that the English have changed the nature of the Pindarries and the Bhils. It is therefore better to suffer the Pindarri peril than that some one else should protect us from it and thus render us effeminate. I should perfer to be killed by the arrow of the Bhil than to seek nominal protection."

When it was pointed out to him that for Home Rule at this stage we have not got an army for our own protection he said the other day :—

"I am here to confess that we are fully able to take charge of all military dispositions in the country and that we feel able to deal with all foreign complications." The worst that may happen is he continued that we may be blotted out from the face of the earth for which he was prepared so long as he can breathe the free atmosphere of India.

The following report is interesting ; we give it below from the "Daily Express."

Q :—Are you anxious to take over the whole control of the army at once or would you make an exception of that object ?

A :—I think we are entirely ready to take up the whole control of the Army which means practically disbanding three fourths of it. I would keep just enough to police India.

Q :—If the army were reduced to that extent, do you not apprehend anything aggressive from the frontier territories ?

A :—No.

Q :—My information, derived from Military sources, is that there are over half-a-million armed men on the frontier.

A :—You are right, I agree.

Q :—These tribes have frequently attacked India hitherto. Why do you think they will refrain from doing so when India possesses Home Rule ?

A :—In the first instance, the world's views have changed and secondly the preparations that are now made in Afghanistan are really in support of the Khilafat. But when the Khilafat question is out of the way, then the Afghan people will not have any design on India. The warrior tribes who live on loot and plunder are given lakhs of rupees as subsidy. I would also give them a little subsidy. When the Charka comes into force in India, I would introduce the spinning wheel among the Afghan tribes also and thus prevent them from attacking the Indian territories. I feel that the tribesmen are in their own way God-fearing people.

But for the fact that he is well known to be a Saint and Mahatma, I would have had no hesitation in saying that his last observations about meeting the Afghans show him to be either a fool or a knave.

He said on the 16th February 1921 :—

"There must be complete independence, if England's policy is in conflict with the Moslim sentiment on the Khilafat question or with the Indian sentiment in the Punjab."

And in his recent speech at the congress opposing the resolution for Independence it was said that if the Punjab and Khilafat demands are complied with, Independence is not necessary. Well, he knows or ought to know they are impossible demands. The implication is plain and taken in conjunction with what has been said above as to the Western civilisation and the Indianisation of the English people, the conclusion that he is really aiming at

Independence is inevitable. To certain Boy Scouts on the 23rd March he was quite plain. He said :—

'No Indian could remain loyal in the accepted sense to the Empire as it was at present represented and be loyal to God at the same time. An Empire that could be responsible for the terrorism of the martial law regime, that would not repent of the wrong, that could enter into secret treaties in breach of solemn obligations could only be reckoned as a Godless Empire. Loyalty to such an Empire was disloyalty to God".

These have to be borne in mind when we consider the question of the Swaraj that he has put forward. The Swaraj that he works for is thus described :—

"Swaraj means full Dominion status. The scheme of such swaraj shall be framed by representatives duly elected in terms of the Congress constitution. That means four anna franchise. Every Indian adult, male or female, paying four annas and signing the Congress creed will be entitled to be placed on the electoral list. These would elect delegates who would frame Swaraj constitution. This shall be given effect to without any change by the British Parliament".

A more preposterous demand cannot be imagined. He excludes all those who do not belong to his Congress. Those who do not pay annas four and sign the congress creed form the majority of the population. Again to ask the British Parliament to accept the scheme framed by his party however absurd, without examination of the same is absolute nonsence. If Mr. Gandhi and his party can frame a scheme of Swaraj for the consideration of the rest of India, have it discussed with others modified if necessary after such discussion, it may be, and it ought to be placed before the Government and Parliament. But this is the last thing he will do, for various reasons. Mr. Gandhi himself will never do it because I doubt whether he has any correct idea of the Dominion status and all that it involves. Mr. Gandhi is not a student but an impulsive fanatic indifferent to facts but obsessed by phantasmagoria. He jumps to what he calls conclusions but which have in fact no premises. Again he will not see it done because what he really desires is not an honest settlement which will give India a further instalment of Swaraj but as the preceeding extracts show what he wants is really absolute independence according to his professions but really anarchy or soul force. If he were honest in his desire to secure Swaraj he and his followers would not have boycotted the Councils but would have entered them to take further steps towards its attainment.

I am therefore satisfied that Mr. Gandhi does not aim at a fair settlement of the Punjab difficulties. He does not want an equitable peace satisfying the just claims of the Mahomedans. He does not want Parliamentary Swaraj or Home Rule But for tactical purposes he is putting them forward to destroy the English Government, in order to attain his object of a society outlined in his "Indian Home Rule," some features of it I have set forth above.—A society without Government, Railways, Hospitals, Schools, Courts. etc. His programme is therefore put forward to clear the way to obtain his object. This Swaraj is to be attained by, in the words of the Resolution, non-violent non-co-operation with Government. And among others the following steps were recommended for adoption: (1) Boycott of Government aided schools and colleges aud establishment of National schools and colleges, (2) Boycott of British Courts by Lawyers and Litigants (3) Boycott of Reformed Councils (4) Boycott of Foreign goods and use of spinning wheels. Out of these I shall naturally take up the question of the boycott of Government and aided institutions and the nature of education sought to be imparted by Mr. Gandhi.

EDUCATION

The system of Education which Mr. Gandhi apparently wants to introduce has already been tried in some parts of India. The results of a teaching confined to Eastern classics and vernaculars has already been apparent. It has produced a mentality amongst Hindus and Mahomedans which has divided them from one another. It has separated still further the Brahmins from non-Brahmins, the caste Hindus from the noncaste Hindus. It has again produced amongst those who have received that education a vague longing for speculative theories and a distaste for experiment and research by which, theories may be tested. Of course Mr. Gandhi does not know these results. His speeches and writings do not show that he ever cared to enquire into these questions. He does not want education to be imparted to the masses and Western education to be imparted to anybody for the reason that it would make them discontented with their present lot in life, *i. e.* in other words he wants each class to remain in its present condition, the lower castes, slaves of their masters—the higher classes. This consequence follows from his acceptance of the caste system. He says "Varanashram (caste system) is inherent in human nature and Hinduism has simply reduced it to a science. It does attach by birth. A man cannot change his Varna by choice. Prohibition against intermarriage and interdining is essential for a rapid evolution of the soul.' He would relegate those Hindus outside the pale of caste, the panchamas or the so-called degraded classes, by whatever name they are called to degradation for the service of the higher castes. His writings or speeches do not show any knowledge of Indian History and having spent the main portion of his life in a far-off country the evils of the system perhaps never came to his knowledge. Otherwise he would have learnt the following facts. It is this caste system which has brought about the conquest of India by the Mahomedans and the Englishmen, both of whom were always supported by the lower castes against the higher.

It is responsible for the large conversions to Christianity and Mahomedanism. It is responsible for a degradation of humanity for which no parallel can be found in slavery, ancient or modern. It is responsible for a good deal of Hindu-Mahomedan, Brahmin non-Brahmin problem and stands in the way of our social, economical and political progress. Yet Mr. Gandhi supports the system, though he advocates the removal of one or two blots which hardly affect the main structure. He enters on an elaborate disquisition on the benefits and necessity of caste which will not do credit to Macaulay's fourth form schoolboy. He shows no knowledge of the vast literature on the subject or of the main arguments against it. He is supporting the caste system to secure the support of the higher castes, without whose financial support his agitation must collapse. One of his own followers would have told him that caste has killed all the arts and science in this country. Sir P. C. Ray points out in his history of Hindu chemistry:— " the fear of losing caste was thus responsible for the loss of the faculty of independent enquiry and hence for the decline and decay of all the arts and sciences for which India was once so famous." Of course he does not want that education which is indispensable for those who occupy the higher Government offices in the country. He does not want that education which is essential for the development of Indian manufacturing industries and development of mineral resources.

Mr. Gandhi accordingly made his wicked attempt to destroy the National Hindu University of Benares and the Mahomedan University of Aligarh. They combined Eastern and Western learning. The attempt was happily unsuccessful. Strong pressure was put upon the students to leave the Schools and Colleges. Looking to the final results as disclosed in the Report of the Congress Secretary reviewing the work of 1921, Government have reasons to congratulate themselves. By far the majority of the aided institutions in Bengal have been recognised by the Educational Authorities to be very inefficient and they have been attempting either to disaffiliate them or reduce their numbers to give more efficient instruction to those who remain, as a good number of them were institutions started for commercial purpose. It is remarkable that the great majority of the students who obeyed the Congress cause belonged to these aided institutions. Those who left the Government Schools and Colleges with better discipline and more efficient teaching were very few if any. I would refer the reader for further information as to the results of the education campaign to the speech of the President of the Thana conference, a genuine patriot who happens, however, to be one of Gandhi's followers. (App. VI).

Mr. Gandhi asked all the boys to withdraw now from the schools on the pretence that until the Government punishes the Punjab offenders in the manner advocated by him and satisfies the claims of the Khilafatists we should no longer associate with the Government, and we can there-by hasten the advent of Swaraj. This is a mere pretext. He advocated the substitution of the national kind of education as outlined by him in favour of the present system of education long before there was any Punjab or Khilafat questions. He advocated them in 1908 in his book "The Indian Home Rule." To say now that he advocated them on account of those reasons is sheer hypocrisy.

The step will not hasten but might retard Swaraj. Even if the Punjab wrongs are redressed in the manner suggested and even if the Khilafatists are satisfied and Parliamentary Swaraj obtained, he will still be an advocate of the abstention from Engligh Schools in favour of the system of national education as above set forth.

VAKILS AND COURTS

The same is the case about his propaganda about the Vakils and the Courts. It never had any chance of success. I shall not dwell however upon this but would refer to Thana President's speech to which in connection with education attention has been already drawn (App. VI). He now puts them forth ostensibly for the purpose of compelling the Government to redress the Punjab and other wrongs. As a fact he advocated them long before that in 1908, as I have already pointed out above. Here again it is sheer hypocrisy to say that they are advocated not as an end in themselves but as a means for the redress of the Punjab and Khilafat wrongs. He dare not openly advocate this as desirable in itself as he would then be laughed at.

BOYCOTT OF COUNCILS

The other step that he advocates is abstention from the new councils. His followers generally have not voted at the elections or have stood for election. His reason given at the Calcutta Congress in September 1920 when he moved his resolution on non-co-operation is this. "I now come to the burning topic *viz.* the boycott of the councils. Sharpest difference of opinion existed regarding this and if the house was to divide on it, it must divide on one viz. whether Swaraj has to be gained through the councils or without the councils. If we utterly distrust the British Government and we know that they are to-day unrepentant now can you believe that the councils will lead to Swaraj and not tighten the British hold on India"? I can only ask him to read the history of the Parliamentary struggle for freedom in England which will show how freedom is won from reluctant monarchs and privileged classes. Even in India the subsequent history of the Legislative councils has shown that the Government is willing to meet the councils half way and almost every question taken up by the councils has been advanced nearer solution. But I doubt whether there is any use of arguing with Mr. Gandhi. The real truth is as he has candidly avowed in his "Indian Home Rule" that Parliamentary Government is in itself bad and India should not strive after it as it will stand in the way of his spiritual Swaraj. I need not argue this point so far as the followers of Gandhi are concerned as they are heartily sorry that they boycotted the councils. I refer on this point also to the Thana Conference President's speech (App. VII). They feel ashamed of themselves the majority of them desire the dissolution of the present councils and a re-election so that they might utilize these councils for more powerful Parliaments. Perhaps I should add that considering the undisciplined fanaticism of the non-co-operator and his total ignorance of development of political organization, it is probably just as well that the councils were in their inception preserved from such a calamitous invasion. The council and the assembly have even in the short duration of their existence, achieved good results which are carrying us far and quietly on that true road to Home Rule from which Mr. Gandhi seeks to divert us. Had the Non Co-operators been members of these councils and had they acted in their present temper, they might well have wrecked the Reforms and have set back the clock of India's progress even more than they have done already. The boycotting is therefore in all probability a blessing though designed as a curse. Still the fact remains that the Councils might have done even more had Mr. Gandhi been endowed with the wisdom to see that India's interests would best be served by using the councils and the assembly as levers to obtain further freedom on sane, safe, and constitutiona llines.

BOYCOTT OF FOREIGN GOODS

There is not only no objection to the Charka but it is very much to be commended. It is very useful as a cottage or home industry and will find an occupation to many who might otherwise be idle. But it will not displace foreign goods at least without the aid of mills by foreign machinery.

All these with other minor ones are only steps to be taken to carry out the policy of non-violent non-co-operation for the attainment of Swaraj and Mr. Gandhi asks every body, in fact the people of India, to carry on non-violent non-co-operation with the Government so as ostensibly to attain Swaraj but really I have no doubt as an end in itself.

I have already pointed out that non-violent submission to suffering and the consequent attainment of self-control over oneself which he called Swaraj was the end which he had in view. He found that there was no use in directly advocating it. He therefore puts it forward as the chief instrument for obtaining the Parliamentary Swaraj which the people of India wanted. He based his appeal to the Hindus on the well known doctrine of "Ahimsa". I will not stop here to discuss how far suffering for the purpose of inducing another to follow a particular line of conduct is included in the scope of Ahimsa. I myself believe it is not only not so included but is totally inconsistent with it. I will merely point out that this principle has already been condemned by the Penal Code which makes it a crime for a creditor to realise his debt by Dhar a. For my purpose it is only necessary to say that this principle of non-violence if accepted in practice generally will lead to chaos and anarchy. If applied to Government alone by refusal to recognise the jurisdiction of the courts it will lead to the same results. How it will lead to 'Parliamentary Swaraj' it is impossible to see. Mr. Gandhi says if all the people of India adopted it the machinery of Government is bound to come to a standstill. But that all will adopt it without leaving sufficient men with the aid of those who will be imported from England and elsewhere to carry out the administration is only the fantasy of a diseased imagination. Non-violence is a guarantee on the part of those who carry it out that the Government has nothing to fear from physical force If they use force then they abandon the weapon of non-violence. Mr. Gandhi and his followers, are agreed that physical force is now out of the question on ground, according to Mr. Gandhi, that we will be crushed. I cannot help thinking that when we take this aspect of the matter along with others already mentioned that Mr. Gandhi himself does not consider this as any effective step towards the attainment of the 'Parliamentary Swaraj,' but only to attain his "Spiritual Swaraj." This explains what he is so fond of reiterating that when Lajpatrai, Motilal Nehru, and C. R. Das and others were arrested and went to Jail without complaint, or resistance denying the jurisdiction of the courts, in pursuance of the policy of non-violent non-co-operation, though Parliamentary Swaraj was not attained, the spiritual 'Swaraj of which he was in search has been attained to his intense satisfaction. If he had advocated abstention from schools, boycott of

Councils and Courts, non-violence as a means of attaining his (spiritual) Swaraj, giving up Punjab Khilafat and Parliamentary Home Rule, no one would perhaps have any right to complain, and it would have been a straightforward and honest course. But he has adopted underhand methods which appear to me, unless a satisfactory explanation is given, little short of dishonest and fraudulent.

But it may be asked whether anybody would have accepted a policy of non-violent non-co-operation in the circumstances of the case unless there was some reasonable prospect of success within any measurable time, Here we come to the most sinister aspect of the matter. In moving his resolution on non-co-operation in the National Congress held at Calcutta in September 1920, he said, "If there is sufficient response to my scheme I make bold to reiterate my statement that you can gain Swarajya in the course of an year" and he laid down certain conditions, the more important of which have been mentioned. That period has been extended subsequently by a few months. Even that extended period has elapsed. When charged with his failure to attain Parliamentary Swaraj within the period asked for by him he had effrontery to state that the conditions mentioned by him have not been complied with. A political leader has no right to put forward before the country any scheme under conditions which he has no reasonable belief of being likely to be complied with. Did he honestly believe that those conditions named by him would be complied with and Parliamentary Swaraj obtained within the time mentioned by him? Looking to the nature of the conditions I do not think he believed that they would be complied with, not only in one year but at any time; and even if complied with I have no doubt he did not believe that Swaraj would come though he might assert the contrary. He put the lure forward simply for the purpose of persuading the Congress to make an important change in the policy which the country had hitherto adopted. The National Congress, carried away by its hostility towards Government, accepted his programme. Some of the younger men may have believed in it. The older and the most experienced I have no doubt never believed in its possibility but considered it a means, of rousing the people of the country from their political lethargy, to put pressure on the Government for further and more extensive reforms. They may also have felt that this might be a means of Mahomedan co-operation for their policy. I do not deny that according to English political life this is a perfectly legitimate manoevre though none of those leaders believed in the soundness of the policy put forward by Mr. Gandhi and many of them said so.

Having attained his purpose by a representation, the truth of which I cannot help thinking he did not believe, and could not have believed, and having committed the Congress to a certain course of action, he is now able to carry the Congress with him for revolutionary action, as it finds it has gone too far on this course to revert to its own natural methods of progress. But as a matter of fact he went further than this.

On 29th December, 1920, *i. e.* three months after the change of programme, he said, "my experience during the last months fills me with the hope that within the nine months that remain of the year in which I have expected Swaraj for India we shall redress the two wrongs and we shall see Swaraj (Parliamentary) established in accordance with the wishes of the people of India." But I do not think for a moment he believed what he said. He used these words to dupe the people of India to follow him yet a step further and to pay him money. After about a month on the 21st of January 1921—he again confirmed his previous statement. He said: "Four months of this one year have already gone by and my faith has never burnt as brightly as it burns to-night as I am talking to the young men of Bengal." And he added "that in case of his death before the expiry of eight months he is satisfied that the people of India will secure Swaraj before the year is out." Is this not a definite statement that the Indian people are going to get Swaraj? A few days later the purpose comes out. In a public address to the merchants of Calcutta on the 30th January, 1921, he said:—

"What I purposed to do I can accomplish in a certain line. I Must attain Swaraj. If thirty crores of people say that they are not with me yet I shall do my work and win Swaraj...If you wish to accomplish work of thirty crores of men then **come out with your money.** Try to have money and ask me to give an account of the same. I appoint some one treasurer...If you know that you yourself can not attain Swaraj then help one with money. If you do not help with money Swaraj will be difficult but not impossible to attain. If the students of India do not help, me it does not matter. If the pleaders do not help, it does not matter.'

The old conditions of the boycott of schools and of the courts as conditions indispensable for the attainment of Swaraj are dropped. And he promises Swaraj and asks for money for getting it in nine months. He collected money on the faith of that representation. Earlier on the same day he got ten thousand rupees, and on the spot a large sum is said to have been collected. On the same date in addressing the students he said. "If the response continues as it has begun there is no doubt of Swaraj coming within the time prescribed". On the 23rd February 1921 he again said: "Last five months experience has confirmed me in the opinion. I am convinced that the country has never been so ready for establishing Swaraj as now." To me only one conclusion is possible that he was collecting the money from the people who understood him to say that Swaraj will be attained within the period mentioned by him. In March he said:

"The last Congress has given a constitution whose working in itself calculated to lead to Swaraj. It is intended to secure in every part of India representative committees working in conjunction with, and under willing and voluntary submission to a central organisation—The all India Congress Committee. It establishes an adult suffrage open to men and women subject only to two qualifications signing of the creed and a nominal payment of four annas. It is intended to secure due representation of the parties and communities, if then, it is honestly worked, and Commands confidence and respect, it can oust the present Government without the slightest difficulty. For, the latter has no power except through the co-operation willing or forced, of the people. The force it exercises is almost through our own people. One lac of Europeans, without our help, can only hold less than one seventh of our villages each and it would be difficult for a man even when physically present, to impose his will on, say four hundred men and women—the average population of Indian village."

He said that we have therefore to concentrate our attention up to the 30th of June on getting :—

(1) One crore of rupees for TilakSwaraj Fund.

(2) One crore members on the Congress register.

(3) The spinning wheel introduced in twenty lacs of homes.

He added, however :

"This programme does not mean cessation of the other activities of Non-co-operation. They go on. Drink and untouchability must vanish. The education movement is steadily going forward. The National institutions that have sprung up will, if they are efficiently managed make headway and attract students who are still hesitating. The pleaders, always a cautious and calculating class by training, will, as they see the movement progressing more and more, fall in line with the rest of the country. Boycott of law courts by the public is making fair progress. These things do not now require concentration of universal effort. They apply to special classes. But the three things mentioned by me are the most essential: they must be done now and without them the movement, as a mass movement must be pronounced a failure. "*Young India*" *30th March*.

After this it is impossible to rely upon boycott of schools &c. as conditions for Swaraj within a year. It is now admitted and the Secretaries report that the money demanded has been collected. Such money was paid on the fraudulent representation of Swaraj within the year. Judged by ordinary standards Mr. Gandhi's whole procedure with the promises, the persuations, the evasions, the subterfuges and all the other manœuvres, would be characterised by men of the world and of sane judgment in language, I hesitate to reproduce, for the simple reason that I believe that Mr. Gandhi is honest in his self hypnotisation. I believe he does not really know what he is doing. At least this is the only possible charitable assumption when we watch his feats of political acrobatics which have the power of deluding such vast numbers of people making them passionately intolerant, violently intolerant often, of the slightest criticism of their hero.

When the Congress was asked in September to change its policy, Mr. Gandhi's idea to start an organisation to supercede the existing Government was not brought before them. It is the first direct step in the path of revolution. His followers have been by this time brought to a proper frame of mind. The use of the money to be collected was, as stated on the 13th April, to be as follows; "The only activity involving financial obligations is that of spinning, organising national service, in some cases supporting lawyers, who might have suspended practice and cannot be included in the national service as for supporting national educational institutions."

It will now be understood why some lawyers were willing to suspend practice. Before the expiry of one year period however other conditions were imposed which would put off Swaraj practically for a very long time to come, the removal of untouchability of the lower classes in India without which it was said Swaraj would be a meaningless term. This means, as I have no doubt, Mr. Gandhi knew, he was putting off Swaraj indefinitely. If this had been mentioned as condition when the Congress was asked to change its policy it is very doubtful whether he would have got the Congress to agree with him. As to these two conditions themselves they are admirable. With a little tact the Government might turn the tables on Mr. Gandhi. If proof of untouchability consists only in the admission of the boys of these classes to schools of higher classes, it does not mean much, though it is a notable advance. If a contact with a low class person is placed on the same footing as contact with caste man it may be said that we have got rid of untouchability. But this will not come throughout the greater portion of India for years. On these questions the education of Mr. Gandhi has only commenced. He will find that without abrogating the ceremonial law on which the caste system rests there will be no practical reform. He is apparently not aware of the far more heinous custom of distance pollution, *i. e.* not only pollution by touch but by approach within a certain distance. This far from being a move against Government would support the Government contention against reform.

About temperance also the move is salutary. If the system of picketting adopted by the volunteers is abandoned and peaceful persuasion alone is attempted no one has any right to complain. What all this has to do with Parliamentary Swaraj or Home Rule one finds it difficult to understand. But they are necessary for the 'Gandhi Swaraj' advocated in his 'Indian Home Rule, and I have little doubt that like his other proposals they were intended to attain that object.

It is admitted in the Report of the Secretaries that the crore of Rupees which was required to be collected, as stated above, has been realised. About the middle of July he said he still looked forward before the next meeting of the Congress for the satisfaction of his demands about the Punjab and the Khilafat and full immediate Swaraj in accordance with the wishes of her chosen representatives. August and September were devoted to the campaign of burning foreign cloth which in his view was an act of non-violent non-co-operation with the Government. This step appeared unintelligible and inacurate to his followers who believed bona fide that he was striving for political control. But it is quite consistent with and in pursuance of his scheme of spiritual swaraj of sacrifice and selfcontrol. On the 27th of October Mr. Gandhi speaks of his "threat to seek the shelter of the Himayalas should violence become universal in India, and should it not have engulfed me."

As *New India* points out: "that would be interesting to know when this threat was made. We all know that Mr. Gandhi said that if there was violence he would go to the Himalayas. There was a riot, but he did not go, but excused himself by saying that if it occurred a second time, he would go. A second riot occured; he said nothing but did not go. Now we hear that he had made a threat to go, should it become universal in India. When and where was this said?"

Towards the end of the month the *Times of India* observed :

> Writing in the latest issue of Navajivan, his Gujarati newspaper, Mr. Gandhi makes the interesting announcement that if Swaraj is not obtained by December, he will either die of a broken heart or retire from public life, leaving the heedless people of India to their resources. Were so clear a pronouncement by any other politician, we could say definitely that when the new year dawns Mr. Gandhi will no longer be actively engaged in politics!"

Can there be any possible doubt that all these statements were made by him in order to impress upon his dupes the fact that they were going to get Swaraj within a year and to deceive his followers to follow him and finance him. Yet what was the situation! Almost every item in his programme has been tried and found useless to attain Home Rule. I would again draw attention to the speech of the President of the Thana District conference for a review of the situation as it then stood in the opinion of one of his prominent followers, (App. VI). This is the opinion of most of his prominent supporters who have been opposing Mr. Gandhi's programme from the very beginning and accordingly the programme was practically shelved and at the Congress held at the end of the year it was resolved to suspend all the activities of the Congress on which stress was much laid. The programme of the volunteer organisation throughout the country was to be carried out on a more extensive scale and the laws of the country were to be defied by disobeying the notifications issued by Government. The Congress also recommended civil disobedience as the only civilised and effective substitute for an armed rebellion and recommended individual disobedience as well as mass civil disobedience when the mass of the people have been sufficiently trained in the practice of non-violence. And the activities of the Congress were to be suspended for that purpose (App. XX). " Offensive civil disobedienee herein recommended is thus defined. *Offensive civil disobedience means " deliberate and wilful breach of State made non-moral laws—that is, laws the breach of which does not involve moral turpitude—not for the purpose of securing the repeal of, or relief from hardships arising from obedience to such laws, but for the purpose of diminishing the authority of, or overthrowing, the State.*"

What took place at the Congress itself was remarkable. The President of the Moslem League, Moulana Hajrat Mohini, who was also a member of the National Congress, proposed his resolution for complete independence. He is reported to have said that although last year they have been promised Swaraj, the redress of the Khilafat and the Punjab wrongs within a year, they had so far achieved nothing (App. XVIII for his view) Mr. Gandhi denied that there was any limitation of one year when the creed was accepted in Nagpur and Calcutta. The special representative of the Congress organ, the *Bombay Chronicle* says: "The feeling in general appear to be in favour of Moulana Hajrat Mohini's resolution" though it was not carried on account of the passionate appeal of Mahatma Gandhi against it. It is instructive to read the resolutions (Appendix XX) that were then passed. Thus Swaraj was to come on September 1-1921, October 31-1921, December 13-1921. At the Congress in December, 1921, Mr. Gandhi gave up fixing any date for the attainment of Swaraj.

The resolution passed in September, 1920, was seditious. The resolution passed in December, 1921, is openly revolutionary, and in fact Gandhi made no secret of it. He says: " Lord Reading must clearly understand that the non-co-operators are at war with the Government. They have declared rebellion against it in as much as it has committed a breach of faith with the Mussalmans. It has humiliated the Punjab and insists upon imposing its will upon the people and refuses to repair the breach and repent for the wrong done in the Punjab " (*Young India.*) Mr. Gandhi also said: "The Government want to goad us into violence or abject surrender. We must do neither. We must retort by such civil disobedience as would campel shooting." The volunteer organizations were pledged to act accordingly. Yet when the Government notified those illegal associations and punished those who defied them, the rebels indignantly remonstrate against what they call coercion and interference with the liberty of person and security of property. They want to be in the limelight to evoke the admiration of America and Europe for their patriotism in rebelling against a Satanic Government. But they are wanting in the redeeming features of these rebels elsewhere —their contempt of danger and death. That is left here to the ignorant masses—the dupes of these men who seek to protect themselves from danger by their doctrine of non-violence.

NON-VIOLENT NON-CO-OPERATION

How on earth is it possible to imagine that all activities would be non-violent when those who are carrying them on proclaim themselves rebels against constitutional authority and are bent upon destroying it; when they say that they must commit civil disobedience of a character that would compel the officials to shoot them! when we know that one large section of it, the Mahomedans, follow a militant religion which not only sanctions but requires them to use force to vindicate what they consider to be their religious law. When we consider further the nature of the activities of those who carry on the Non-co-operation movement there can be still less room to doubt that riots ending in bloodshed are bound to follow. In order to carry out the Non-co-operation campaign India is divided into various Congress provinces. Congress committees are formed consisting of members who are also pledged to carry out the Congress principles: there are also volunteer organizations formed. The function of these bodies is to impress upon the people of the country the enormity of Government's crime with reference to the Punjab and the Khilafat and the consequent necessity of Home Rule or Swaraj. For attaining such Swaraj they advocate progressive non-co-operation by "peaceful" methods. Such methods consist of various steps which are described in the speech of Mr. Macpherson, extracted below. Starting, perhaps, peacefully they soon exhibit a tendency to violence and when Mahomedan sentiments are involved, when appeals are made to Mahomedan religious feelings, that tendency becomes almost irresistible in their case. Opposition to constituted authority inflames them into violence and instead of submitting to violence at the hands of authorities according to the dictates of Gandhi—a counsel of perfection—they retort—and murder is the result. The process is so well put by Mr. Macpherson in the Behar Legislative Council that I take the liberty of quoting the following extract from his speech:—

"It is necessary to consider what is the essence of

the non-co-operation movement, what are its ultimate objects and what are its methods. From the moment Mr. Gandhi first unfolded his plan of compaign—that was, I think, at a Benares or Allahabad Conference in 1920—there has never been any doubt in my mind that the objects of the movement were entirely unconstitutional, that its methods were illegal and that its prosecution to the bitter end is bound to result in violence, disorder and anarchy, however much non-violence may be proclaimed as the watchword of its leaders. The movement cannot be judged by its earlier and comparatively innocuous stages, as if these stood by themselves. 1 refer to the resignation of titles, the boycott of Government schools and colleges the abandonment of their profession by legal practitioners and other such manifestations of non-co-operation, although all these items in the programme have done an infinite amount of harm, especially to the youth. of the country, and even these earlier stages have been marked by repeated outbursts of violence, by a concerted system of intimidation and social boycott, and by the excitement of racial hatred which has had deplorable results in individual cases. No, the plan of compaign must be taken as a whole, and judged by its closing stages, the enforcement of civil disobedience towards the laws of the country, interference with the police and the judicial administration, the invasion of police stations, picketting of Courts, the seduction of the troops from their allegiance. and the refusal to pay taxes or rent or revenue. The movement must indeed be judged by its ultimate object, which is the paralysis and subversion of the existing Government and by its inevitable result, general disorder and bloodshed and widespread misery amongst all classes and communities. If pursued to the bitter end, it will assuredly have this result, whether it succeeds or fails, and should it (which God forbid) succeed, the end can only be a state of chaos which will make India the prey of the violent tribes that dwell around her borders or the hungry hordes of Central Asia who, in the course of history, have more than once invaded India. *The object of the movement being what it is, the overthrow of the existing Government in India, what is the use of telling us that either its leaders or its followers have signed a pledge of non-violence? The pledge is a farce; it has already been broken a hundred times over, and the longer the movement continues and the further it advances, the more it will be broken.*"

That this has been the case is illustrated by almost all the riots which have taken place. Malabar stands first in its unenviable notoriety. There the Congress committees were formed; the Khilafat committees also were formed; Gandhi and Shaukat Ali visited Malabar, preached their sermons and the usual result followed. With Mahomedans Swaraj was only their secondary aim, their principal object being the redress of the Khalif's wrongs and the establishment of a Khilafat kingdom in the country. When, therefore, the British Government interfered with the activities of some of the Khilafat leaders the Mohomedan population as a whole rose in rebellion and invited the Hindus ; to join them. The Hindus as a body remained loyal ; and the results were disastrous both to the Mahomedans and to the Hindus, more than two thousand Mahomedans killed by troops according to official estimates, thousands more in other ways ; far larger numbers wounded ; the number of Hindus butchered in circumstances of barbarity, flayed alive, made to dig their own graves before slaughter, running into thousands ; women and purdah women too, raped, not in a fit of passion but systematically for months passed from hand to hand and with calculated revolting and horrible cruelty for which I have not been able to find a parallel in history. Thousands were forcibly converted. All this done in the name of, and to enforce, the Khilafat movement : all this due directly to the visit of Gandhi and Shaukat Ali and to the organization of Khilafat associations. They carried on their activities openly without any obstruction by the authorities; the Government of Madras was prevented from interfering with Khilafat agitators by the Government of India who are therefore as responsible as if they had directly ordered all this frightfulness.

I take the United Provinces next and will refer not only to the activities of the volunteers but to the entire situation as it developed itself from the commencement of the year 1921. That will also show the earnest efforts which were made by the Government to co-operate with the constitutional party to work the Reform Scheme in a sympathetic spirit.

In welcoming the Legislative Council on the 22nd of January, 1921, Sir Harcourt Butler drew attention to the great efforts which were being made by Mr. Gandhi's party to achieve their objects, to their aim, to their failure till that time to achieve any appreciable success. (App. VII) By March the situation had become worse and he narrated the circumstances which compelled him to extend the Seditious Meetings Act to some of the districts. (App. VIII) By the end of the year the situation became intolerable. Sir Harcourt Butler has described the efforts of the Non-co-operators, and the success they have achieved, in his speech on the 17th December 1921. (App. IX).

And finally Sir Ludovic Porter, a member of the Government, described the whole situation, including the various efforts that were being made by the Non-co-operators on the 23rd of January 1922. (App. X). This will explain also the nature of the associations of volunteers formed under the Resolution of the Congress already referred to, their efforts and their illegal character. And more recently we now hear of far more serious disturbances in Gorakhpur where a mob of volunteers and villagers about 2000 in number led by the former killed 21 policemen and chowkidars (App. XII) and at Rai Bareilly where there was a serious collision. In order to understand the *modus operandi* I give an official narrative of the events at Barabanki. (App. XI) About Behar we have the speech of Mr. Machpherson, a member of Council, in which he refers to the plans of the non-co-operation party to win Swaraj, gives the organization of the national volunteers describes how the Government offices were to be taken possession of, civil disobedience was to be started, gives the deplorable conditions in various districts brought about by the non-co-operation campaign and describes the revolutionary character of the movement in that province. (App. XVI). The chief secretary, Mr. Hammond, in his speech gives various instances of tyranny practised by the non-co-operation volunteers, a practical speech which proves his contention (App. XVII). In Bengal, on Nov. 20 Lord Ronaldshay drew attention to the nature of Gandhi Swaraj and Turkish administration (App. XIII). In Nov. 1921, he spoke about the intended boycott of the Prince of Wales (App. XIII). In another speech he pointed out the lies that were being spread about the bombardment of Mecca (App. XIII). In Dec. 1921, he described the activities which led to the interference of Government. A brief extract will be found in (App. XII). Finally, in Feb. 1922, he made a lengthy reference to the political outlook (App. XIII). In the Legislative Council Sir. Henry Wheeler a member of Government described the situation (App. XV.)

In the Legislative Assembly also the matter was fully discussed in Jan. 1922. Sir William Vincent summed up the situation, various instances of their activities among which will be found a particularly revolting statement about the corpse of a diseased person who was loyal to the Government, and therefore obnovious to Gandhi's party, being dug out of the grave. (App. XXIII).

This completes my review of the situation. Considerations of space have compelled me to exclude many speeches which would throw further light on the situation.

I will, therefore, content myself with giving a list of the disturbances and riots throughout India, due to Gandhi's movement supplied to me by the Legislative Department of the Government of India. (App. XXII).

In February 1922 Mr. Gandhi issued an ultimatum to the Government of India that if within a certain period of time his demands formulated in his ultimatum were not conceded he would start what is called mass civil disobedience at Bardoli, that is to say, the people of Bardoli would be asked to refuse to pay taxes etc. The Government of India issued a communique in reply in which reviewing the situation they pointed out the grave dangers that would follow such civil disobedience and gave him a stern warning. (App. XIX).

This attitude no doubt surprised him. The Government he thought was on the run, when they had submitted meekly to his contemptuous refusal for a conference at Calcutta and he had apparenly therefore expected them to beg for an armistice. There was a remarkable change. He or rather the working committee of the Congress suspended mass civil disobedience having found a pretext in the occurrence of a riot about this time at Gorakhpur. So far as the campaign against the Government is concerned the following are the important resolutions :—

"The working Committee of the Congress resolves that mass civil disobedience contemplated at Bardoli and elsewhere be suspended and instructs the local Congress Committees forthwith to advice the cultivators to pay the land revenue and other taxes due to the Government and whose payment might have been suspended in anticipation of mass civil disobedience and instructs them to suspend every other preparatory activity of an offensive nature." "The suspension of mass civil disobedience shall be continued till the atmosphere is so non-violent as to ensure the non-repetition of popular atrocities such as at Gorakhpur, or hooliganism such as at Bombay and Madras respectively on the 17th November, 1921 and 13th January last. In order to promote a peaceful atmosphere the working Committee advises till further instruction, all Congress organisations to stop activities specially designed to court arrest and imprisonment, save normal Congress activities including voluntary hartals wherever an absolutely peaceful atmosphere can be assured, and for that end all picketting shall be stopped save for the bona fide and peaceful purpose of warning the visitors to liquor shops against the evils of drinking. Such picketting to be controlled by persons of known good character and specially selected by the Congress Committee concerned."

"The working Committe advises, till further instructions, the stoppage of all volunteer processions and public meetings merely for the purpose of defiance of the notification regarding such meetings. This, however, shall not interfere with the private meetings of the Congress and other committees or public meetings which are required for the conduct of the normal activities of the Congress".

The working Committee advised all Congress organisations to be engaged in the following activities:—

"To enlist at least one crore of members of the Congress. The workers should note that no one who does not pay the annual subcription can be regarded as a qualified congressman."

" To continue the Swarja fund and to call upon every Congressman or Congress-sympathiser to pay at least one hundreth part of his annual income for the year 1921. Every province to send every month 25 per cent of its income from the Tilak Memorial Swaraj fund to the All India Congress Committee."

The above resolutions were directed to be placed before the All-India Congress Committee for revision if necessary. They were accordingly brought before the All-India Congress Committee whose Resolution runs thus.

" The All-India Congress Committee havive carefully considred the resolutions passed by the Working Committee at its meeting held at Bardoli on the 11th and 12th instant, confirms the said resolutions with the modifications noted herein and *further resolves that individual civil dis-obence whether of a defensive or aggressive charecter, may be commenced in respect of particular places or particular laws, at the instance of, and upon permission being granted therefore, by the respective provincial Committee.*

Provided that such civil disobedience shall not be permitted unless all the conditions laid down by the Congress or the All India Congress Commitee or the Working Committee are strictly fulfilled.

Reports having been received from various quarters that picketting regarding foreign cloth is as necessary as liquor picketting, the All-India Congress Committee *authorises such picketing* of a bona fide character on the same terms as liquor picketing mentioned in the Bardoli resolutions.

The All-India Congress Committee wishes it to be understood that the resolutions of the Working Committee do not mean an abandonment of the original Congress programme of non-co-operation or the permanent abandonment of mass civil disobedience, but considers that an atmosphere of necessary mass non-violence can be established by the workers concentrating upon the constructive programme framed by the Working committee at Bardoli. The All-India Congress Committee holds civil *disobedience to be the right and duty of the people to be exercised and performed whenever the State opposed the declared will of the people.*

INDIVIDUAL CIVIL DISOBEDIENCE

Note.—Individual civil disobedience is disobedience of orders or laws by a single individual or an ascertained number or group of individuals. Therefore, a prohibited public meeting where admission is regulated by tickets and to which no unauthorised admission is allowed, is an instance of individual civil disobedience whereas a prohibited meeting to which the general public is admitted without any restriction, is an instance of mass civil disobedience.

Such civil disobedience is defensive, when a prohibited public meeting is held for conducting a normal activity although it may result in arrest. It would be aggressive, if it is held, not for any activity, but merely for the purpose of courting arrest and imprisonment."

This shows that there is practically no change in the situation. This may be read with the resolution of the congress 28th Dec. 1921. (App. XX). Gandhi's agitation continues revolutionary.

For more than thirty years the constitutional Reform party have been fighting for various indispensable reforms in the administration of the country with but moderate success. At last however, in 1919 they obtained a Reform scheme which brought India directly on to the path leading to Home Rule. In fact the Reform Act made Home Rule inevitable within a comparatively short time, and indicated the nature of the constitutional methods of its early attainment. Mr. Gandhi was in India for some years before that date. He scarcely lent any assistance to the Reform party. Considering his principles he could not. After having obtained the Act, the Reform party proceeded to work it, to carry out the administrative reforms needed, to educate the masses to enable them to claim and exercise larger political powers, in order to claim at as early a date as possible that further instalment of Reform provided for and contemplated in the act itself. Mr. Gandhi is standing right athwart their path, thus preventing or at least retarding and dangerously imperilling the indispensable reforms, regardless of the sufferings of the people entailed thereby, in order to carry out his own wild principles which have not the slightest chance of acceptance provided they are understood by the people of the country for what they are, emotional speculations without any considered relation to existing conditions. Mr. Gandhi, to take him at his best is indifferent to facts. Facts must submit to the dictates of his theories. The only difficulty in his way is that they don't. Will o'the wisp politics are not of use to a people who have to live in a world which, from long and bitter experience, has at last come to realise that dreams of distarted brains are not the stuff of which contented Nations are made. Gandhi in fact is seeking not only to destroy the fruits of the long endeavour of the constitutional reformers, but blast for ever any hopes of Indian regeneration.

To push forward the working of the Act has been the work before the Reform party which he is thus so perniciously thwarthing. They had to take up in the Legislative Councils the question of the redress of the grievances under which the people suffered, not only to agitate for their removal, but to show the people that by constitutional agitation sooner or later they can get what they want. The most important question with which the constitutional Reformers had to deal was one concerning the great poverty of the country. For this it is necessary to consider the quesion of the Land Tax—its nature, incidents, relation to other taxes, its necessity, the distribution of the land produce between the Government and the classes that own the land. This is a question in which the landholding classes are very much interested. They would have understood the arguments addressed to them and therefore it would have served as a means of political and social education. The Councils have already been dealing with it, and, considering the conditions, satisfactorily. The Government have been meeting them in a sympathetic spirit and are trying to give effect to their proposals as much as possible. What is Mr. Gandhi's advice? He does not seek to co-operate to make the tax less oppressive. He would have the people pay no land tax to Government. Only the dreadful consequences that would ensue prevent him in this case, from giving full effect to his intentions. In any case, it is not the oppressive nature of the tax that he relies on, nor is it alleged that it is an innovation of the British Government, which of course it is not. He objects to the tax, not for itself, but because it is another weapon with which to destroy the Government.

A cognate question is that which arises between the landlords and tenants. In this also all the landholding classes are deeply interested, and a discussion of the nature of the distribution of the produce between the landlord, farmer and agricultural labourer would have been of great educative value. The Legislative Councils are dealing with the question. Government in this matter also are showing the greatest possible consideration for the feelings of the people of the country. Yet Mr. Gandhi and his friends would not only take no part in the deliberations of the council but would prevent an amicable settlement by steps which have produced riots between the classes interested in the land, with the object of discrediting the Reform Scheme and paralysing the Government of the country.

Closely connected with this is the question of Indian manufactures, industries and the development of mineral resources, which, besides, conferring other benefits, will relieve undue pressure on the land. Our industries have been destroyed by English competition and constitutional reformers are determined to take all the steps necessary to enter into healthy competition with English industries in Indian interests and to develop their own mineral and other.resources. In so doing they have to take care that the conditions which accompanied the rise of industrial prosperity in the West are not reproduced in India. They have to see that wage earners received adequate protection. What are the tactics of Mr. Gandhi and his friends? All these industries are to him the devil's-own agency to destroy the soul. He says they cannot add an inch to India's moral stature. Starvation due to the absence of industries may destroy the body and certainly hinders the development of the soul. But to him this does not matter. He and his followers would taboo machinery, without which competition or development is hopeless. Without attempting to promote an amicable settlement between English capitalists and Indian labourers they have on the contrary been responsible for a deliberate widening of the chasm between the races.

The administration of justice is another matter in which all are interested ; and already the Legislative Councils are dealing with the question of the separation of Judicial and Executive functions. The Government again are not only not standing in their way but are rendering every assistance towards the solution of the problem. This is also the case with reference to the removal of discriminations between Europeans and Indians in the administration of justice. The people of the country understand this question well as they are deeply interested in it. Mr. Gandhi is asking the people of the country to avoid all courts and thus not to interest themselves in the improvement of judicial administration.

I might take many other questions relating to finances, army, etc, and show the baneful influence of his propaganda. In all these Mr. Gandhi's compaign against Government has hampered the reformers who would otherwise have made the redress of these grievances a more effective plank in their platform ; these questions would have been more widely discussed throughout the country. But such discussion is now almost impossible with the result that these questions are not settled as satisfactorily as they might otherwise be. But it is as regards education that the reformers have most felt the want of that popular support necessary to carry out the reforms needed.

Mr. Gandhi will never be forgiven by all true lovers of sound National Education for India for the campaign he has carried on against real education. The education that has been hitherto imparted had been as everybody, including Mr. Gandhi also recognised, lamentably defective. The reformers had to insist on the imparting of suitable primary education to the masses, to the workers, to the labouring men and others, to enable them to improve their condition, because no class can generally rise except under the ultimate stress of its own will and ability. They had to demand suitable higher education, which was required not only in the interests of the culture but also for the industrial regeneration of the country and for the development of India's natural resources. In the laboratories of Europe, America and Japan students are devoting themselves to discover means for the alleviation of misery and pain. Nay, higher claims are advanced, for it has been declared by scientists that we are on the eve of discovery of means for a practically indefinite prolongation of life under certain conditions which make us intensely expectant to know whether they are the same as described in our ancient books as efficacious for that purpose, descriptions which have hitherto been contemptuously discarded as worthless. Archaelogists are almost every day unveiling to us ancient remains and writings which give us a different and a startling conception of ancient History and Civilisation. Indian History is being rewritten. When we hear of the Marconi wireless, our young men turn to our own ancient descriptions of the training of human body and mind which make these fit to receive and convey messages regardless of space and distance and they show eagerness to take part in experiment and research. When we find rays penetrating solid matter, our young scientists wonder whether after all the stories of great seers whose vision, not of the material eye, is not bounded by time or space or distance, may not be true and wonder whether we should not now take up the training prescribed to attain those results. Researches are made in the laboratories to control the forces of nature, to increase human comforts and happiness, to increase productivity in all directions. Researches have already attained brilliant results. The lessons of the survey of the regions above by the telescope, of all below by the miscroscope, and generally speaking all these marvels of science which lend fresh light and new significance to the lesson of ancients as to the all pervading of the universe are all anathema to Mr. Gandhi.

He wants to hold back our boys from the Universities and post-graduate studies and research that they may go back to their ploughs while the Uuiversities of the Western world are sending their delegates all over the world to take stock of what has been done and to devise means for the intellectual and moral uplift of the Nations.

The constitutional reformers and the Councils have the great task before them of reconciling the Hindus and Mahomedans on a basis for their unity other than the one which arose out of the Mahomedan fury against the British Government for its failure to support Mahomedan interests in the West.

They have also to promote goodwill between the Hindus and the Mahomedans on the one side and the Europeans on the other, both in India and in the colonies. They have to face the rising antagonism between the dark, the fair and the white—an antagonism which threatens in course of time to engulf the whites with all that modern civilisation, whatever be its faults, is standing for. The Reform party want India to take her rightful place in the Indo-British commonwealth, the first place, in fact, to which her natural genius and her resources entitle her, with all its responsibilities. The conditions are all favourable to India. Governorships of Provinces are thrown open to Indians. There are Indians in the Viceroy's and other Councils. But Mr. Gandhi and his friends will not only do practically nothing in that direction but they have created what threatens to be a permanent gulf between the Mahomedans and non-Mahomedans, and they are dangerously widening the gulf between the Indians and Europeans. The reformers have to improve the conditions of women both amongst the Mahomedans and the Hindus, as without such improvement India is not entitled to take her place among civilised nations. They have practically to get rid of the caste system as with such a cancer political progress is impossible. Mr. Gandhi, on the other hand, panders to Mahomedan vanity and justifies the racial differences as between different classes of Hindus. He insists upon the necessity of our going back to our own caste system, which is responsible for the condition of our women and of the lower classes. He has given a handle to those who want to maintain the repressive laws, and is really responsib'e for the retention of them. He has not only thrown doubts as to our fitness for Self-Government but has rendered it possible for our opponents to urge with plausibility that danger would accrue to the Empire and to India itself by granting Home Rule to India. He has thus to the best of his sinister ability attempted to prevent all reforms and has tried to paralyse all the efforts of the reformers in every direction, fomenting racial and class differences, as I have already explained.

Everywhere we see a class of narrow thought in the white world raising the colour sentiment against the Asiatics, and against

Indians in particular, proclaiming that there is no place for Indians in British Empire on terms of equality. These are not the intellectual leaders of the white races, nor are they those who set the best standards of morality. On the other hand, we see the noblest of them proclaiming and striving with all their might, with varying degrees of success, to enforce the opposite ideal. We know also that in India the question is only one of time and within a short period absolute equality in every respect will be carried out. We see further that our countrymen elsewhere are weak and comparatively helpless, and till we in India attain our manhood they must continue at the mercy of the white races. What is it, then, that not only Religion, Universal morality, or good, but also policy and prudence, dictate? There can be only one answer. We must strengthen the hands of those who are fighting for race equality and give no opportunity to those who maintain that the Indians are a peril to the white race. What is Mr. Gandhi doing? He is doing everything possible to increase racial and class hatred.

We see the wonderful phenomenon of

Australian ladies begging pardon for the atrocious treatment of their Indian sisters by a few Englishmen in Fiji and elsewhere. We see the Universities and Professors, ashamed of themselves for their aberration during the great War, hastening to make amends by trying to bring together all classes and races of men. We see white women trying to band themselves and other women of whatever colour and creed into one sisterhood, without any difference, to throw themselves into all social and political movements for sex enfranchisement and uplift; to work for the good not only of themselves but of children in particular, and generally to devote themselves to all activities of mercy. We find various Nations calling to one another across seas, deserts and mountains to join in a common fellowship, not to work in opposition to one another. Every where, after the fearful cataclysm through which we have passed, there is wistful yearning for fellowship and brother-hood to carry out in practice the teachings of the ancient prophets and seers, Buddha, Confucius, Zoroaster, the seers of the Upanishads, Christ, Mahomed, in opposition to the Churches and the dogmatic religions identified with their names. And is it not extraordinary, we see this man, uninfluenced by this tremendous intellectual and moral up-heaval, waging a bloody and racial struggle for what? that if successful Indians may not take part in any of these movements, shun them all, since God has not created man with his limited means of natural locomotion to labour for general good, and may therefore, retire to their village to lead a solitary life.

If he had followed this advice for himself, or had retired to the Himalayas to live a mahatmaic life he would have saved the lives literally of thousands, prevented horrible outrages worse than death, saved thousands from incalculable misery. Instead of paying the penalty themselves, he and his lieutenants stalk about the country dripping with the blood of the victims of their policy.

Who is responsible for all this? The Government of India cannot divest themselves of their responsibility and India will hold the Indian members primarily responsible for the present situation. For no Viceroy will venture to disregard their advice in a matter of this sort. They do not seem to have strengthened the fibre of the Government. Nor have the Legislative Councils who also must share the responsibility advanced the claim for the transfer of the administration of justice to popular control. The Gandhi movement will no doubt collapse by internal disruption as it is composed of various elements, drawn from Tolstoy Lenin communism, socialism, Rigid Brahmanism, millitant Mahomedanism mutually repellent and explosive when they come into contact with one another and already producing the natural terrible results. But before the final collapse comes it will have produced appalling misery and bloodshed unless it is dealt with firmly and with statesmanship. The Government should give Mr. Gandhi and some of his chief lieutenants who accept the whole programme the rest, they sadly need. And the Congress and the Khilafat associations must be treated as they themselves wish to be treated as disloyal illegal associations.

Since the above lines were written Mr. Gandhi has been arrested. tried and convicted. He pleaded guilty to the charges framed against him. His statements are worthy of careful attention. (App XXI) He said " I wish to endorse all the blame that the learned Advocate-General has thrown on my shoulders in connection with the Bombay occurrences, Madras occurrences and the Chauri Chaura occurrences. Thinking over these deeply and sleeping over them night after night, it is impossible for me to dissociate myself from the diabolical crimes of Chauri Chaura or the mad outrages of Bombay." He is quite right when he says, that "as a man of responsibility, a man having received a fair share of education, having had fair share of experience of this world, I should have known the consequences of every one of my acts. *I knew that I was playing with fire. I ran the risk and if I was set free I would still do the same.* I have felt it this morning that I would have failed in my duty, if I did not say what I said here just now." A man who says that if set free he would still pursue the same course though aware of the consequences of his acts is not a safe leader. There are signs however of a general recognition throughout the country that Mr. Gandhi's theories are no longer suitable as a guide for political action. The Maharashtra party have apparently resolved to seek admission into the

Legislative councils. The Central Provinces are also apparently of the same opinion. A large section of Bengal represented by the Chitagong conference apparently hold the same view. In Madras a considerable section is inclined to agree. But there is little doubt that it would take a long time to erradicate the feeling of hatred that has been roused by Mr. Gandhi throughout the country.

As I left the Government of India long before the campaign of non-co-operation was launched, perhaps there is nothing inappropriate in the few observations which I propose to make regarding the delay in taking action against Mr. Gandhi and his followers. In September 1920 the Congress adopted the non-co-operation resolution. The Government might then have taken action with the support of a large majority of Indian politicians. After the final adoption of a non-co-operation programme by the Nagpur Congress it was felt that the Government should have stopped the activities of the party which from that moment had openly declared their disloyalty. They maintained their silence however even after Gandhi and the Congress party resolved on the recruitment of volunteers and the organisation of a parallel Government. On the arrest and trial of the Ali Brothers Mr. Gandhi challenged the Government to arrest him as he maintained that the conduct of the Ali Brothers in tampering with the loyalty of the Sepoys and uttering sedition was only in pursuance of the policy adopted by himself and the congress. His words are remarkable. "The National Congress began to tamper with the loyalty of the sepoys in September last year, i. e. 1920 the Central Khilafat Committee began it earlier and I began it earlier still, for I must be permitted to take the credit or the odium of suggesting, that India had a right openly to tell the sepoy and everyone who served the Government in any capacity whatsoever that he participated in the wrongs done by the Government."—"Every non-co-operator is pledged to preach disaffection towards the Government established by law. Non-co-operation, though, a religious and strictly moral movement, deliberately aims at the overthrow of the Government, and is therefore legally seditious in terms of the Indian Penal Code. But this is no new discovery.

Lord Chelmsford knew it. Lord Reading knows it" .... " we must reiterate from a thousand platforms the formula of the Ali Brothers regarding the sepoys, and we must spread disaffection openly and systemtically till it pleases the Government to arrest us." It will hardly be believed that even after this no steps were taken against him. Towards the end of the year he said " Lord Reading must clearly understand that the no-co-operators are at war with the Government. They have declared rebellion against it." It was after this that there was an attempt to bring abut a conference between him and the Government which was contemptuously brushed aside by him. One of the mopla leaders when tried for rebellion pleaded that he was under the impression that the British Government no longer ruled the country and had abdicated. There is very little doubt of the unfortunate fact that there was a general belief that the Government was powerless and could be safely defied by Gandhi and his congress.

APPENDIX I

VICEROY'S SPEECH.

"A few Europeans and many Hindus, have been murdered, communications have been obstructed, Government offices burnt and looted and records have been destroyed, Hindu temples sacked, houses of Europeans and Hindus burnt, according to reports Hindus were forcibly converted to Islam and one of the most fertile tracts of South India is faced with certain famine. The result has been the temporary collapse of the Civil Government, the offices and Courts have ceased to function and ordinary business has been brought to a standstill. European and Hindu refugees of all classes are concentrated at Calicut and it is satisfactory to note that they are safe there. One trembles to think of the consequences if the forces of order had not prevailed for the protection of Calicut. The non Muslim in these parts was fortunate indeed that either he or his family or his house or property came under the protection of the soldiers and the police. Those who are responsible for causing this grave outbreak of violence and crime must be brought to justice and made to suffer the punishment of the guilty.

Effect of violent preaching

"But apart from direct responsibility, can it be doubted that when poor unfortunate and deluded people are led to believe that they should disregard the law and defy authority, violence and crime must follow? This outbreak is but another instance on a much more serious scale and among a more turbulent and fanatical people, of the conditions that have manifested themselves at times in various parts of the country and, gentlemen, I ask myself and you and the country generally what else can be the result from instilling such doctrines into the minds of the masses of the people? How can there be peace and tranquility when ignorant people, who have no means of testing the truth of the inflamatory and too often deliberately false statements made to them, are thus misled by those, whose design is to provoke violence and disorder. Passions are thus easily excited to unreasoning fury.

The Leader of the Movement

"Although, I freely acknowledge that the leader of the movement to paralyse authority, persistently, and, as I believe, in all earnestness and sincerity, preaches the doctrine of non-violence and has even reproved his followers-for resorting to it, yet again and again it has been showed that his doctrine is completely forgotten and his exhortations absolutely disregarded when passions are excited as must inevitably be the consequence among emotional people.

Its inevitable result

"To those who are responsible for the peace and good government of this great Empire and I trust that to all men of sanity and common sense in all classes of society, it must be clear that the defiance of the Government and constituted authority can only result in widespread disorder, in political chaos, in anarchy and in ruin".

APPENDIX II

DIABOLICAL ATROCITIES.

Calicut, Sept. 7—In my first article I dealt with the prime causes of the present outbreak, the dangerous game played by the leaders of the Khilafat and Non-Co-operation movements in Malabar which set the whole of Ernad and Walluvanad ablaze, and the extent of plunders, murders and forcible conversions committed by the Mopla rebels. In this article I intend to confine myself to the nature of the atrocities committed by them and other details.

The experiences I am about to relate will satisfy every Hindu endowed with ordinary common sense that the Moplas resorted to most repugnant fanaticism, which may be ascribed to nothing but selfishness, love of money and love of power, which are the prominent features of the present outbreak. Refugees narrate that, after forcibly removing young and fair Nair and other high caste girls from their parents and husbands, the Mopla rebels stripped them of their clothing and made them march in their presence naked, and finally they committed rape upon them. In certain instances, devoid of human feelings and blinded by animal passion, the Moplas are alleged to have utilised a single woman for the gratification of the carnal pleasures of a dozen or more men. The rebels also seem to have captured beautiful Hindu women, forcibly converted them, pierced holes in their ears in the typical Mopla fashion, dressed them as Mopla women and utilised them as their temporary partners in life. Hindu women were threatened, molested and compelled to run half-naked for shelter to forests abounding in wild animals. Respectable Hindu gentlemen were forcibly converted and the circumcision ceremony performed with the help of certain Musaliars and Thangals. Hindu houses were looted and set fire to, will not all these atrocities remain as a shameful image of the Hindu Muslim "unity", of which we have heard much from the Non-Co-operation Party and Khilafat-wallahs? The ghastly spectacle of a number of Hindu damsels being forced to march naked in the midst of a number of licentious Moplas cannot be forgotten by any self respecting Hindu, nor can it be erased from their minds. On the other hand, I have never heard of the modesty of a Mopla woman being outraged by a Mopla rebel. "*Times of India*."

APPENDIX III

MALABAR'S AGONY.

By Annie Besant

It would be well if Mr. Gandhi could be taken into Malabar to see with his own eyes the ghastly horrors which have been created by the preaching of himself and his "loved brothers," Muhommad and Shaukat Ali. The Khilafat Raj is established there; on August 1, 1921, sharp to the date first announced by Mr. Gandhi for the beginning of Swaraj and the vanishing of British Rule, a Police Inspector was surrounded by Moplas, revolting against that Rule. From that date onwards thousands of the forbidden war-knives ware secretly made and hidden away, and on August 20, the rebellion broke out, Khilafat flags were hoisted on Police Stations and Government offices. Strangely enough it was on August 25th 825 A. D. that Cherman Perumal ascended the throne of Malabar, the first Zamorin, and from that day the Malayalam Era is dated that is still in use; thus for 1096 years a Zamorin has ruled in Calicut, and the Rajas are mostly Chiefs who for long centuries have looked to a Zamorin as their feudatory Head. These are the men on whom the true pacification of Malabar must ultimately depend. The crowded refugees will only return to their devastated homes when they see those once more in safety in their ancestral places. Their lands, which they keep under their own control, are largely cultivated by Moplas, who are normally hardy, industrious agricultural labourers.

Our correspondent has sent accounts of the public functions connected with my hurried visit to Calicut and Palghat, and that which I wish to put on record here is the ghastly misery which prevails, the heart-breaking wretchedness which has been caused by the Mopla outbreak, directly due to the violent and unscrupulous attacks on the Government made by the Non-Co-operators and the Khilafatists and the statements scattered broadcast, predicting the speedy disappearance of British Rule, and the establishment of

Swaraj, as proclaimed by the N. C. O. and Khilafat Raj. as understood by the Moplas from the declarations of the Khilafatists. On that, there is no doubt whatever, so far as Malabar is concerned. The message of the Khilafats, of England as the enemy of Islam, of her coming downfall, and the triumph of the Muslims, had spread, to every Mopla home. The harangues in the Mosques spread it everywhere, and Muslim hearts were glad. They saw the N.C.O., preachers appealing for help to their religious leaders, naturally identified the two. The Government was Satanic, and Eblis, to the good Muslim, is to be fought to the death. Mr. Gandhi may talk as he pleases about N. C. O.s accepting no responsibility. It is not what they accept ; it is what facts demonstrate. He accepted responsibility for the trifling bloodshed of Bombay. The slaughter in Malabar cries out his responsibility. N. C. O. is dead in Malabar. But bitter hatred has arisen there, as fighting men from the dragon's teeth of Theseus. That is the ghastly result of the preaching of Gandhism, of N. C. O. of Khilafatism. Every one speaks of the Khilafat Raj, and the one hope of the masses is in its crushing by the strong arm of the Government. Mr. Gandhi asks the Moderates to compel the Government to suspend hostilities, *i. e.*, to let loose the wolves to destroy what lives are left. The sympathy of the Moderates is not, I make bold to say, with the murderers, the looters, the ravishers, who have put into practice the teachings of paralysing the Government of the N. C. O.'s, who have made " war on the Government " in their own way. How does Mr. Gandhi like the Mopla spirit, as shown by one of the prisoners in the Hospital, who was dying from the results of asphyxiation ? He asked the surgeon, if he was going to die, and surgeon answered that he feared he would not recover, " Well, I'm glad I killed fonrteen infidels," said the ' Brave, God-fearing Mopla, whom Mr. Gandhi so much admires, who " are fighting for what they consider as religion, and in a manner they consider as religious." Men who consider it "religious" to murder, rape, loot, to kill women and little children, cutting down whole families, have to be put under restraint in any civilised society.

Mr. Gandhi was shocked when some Parsi ladies had

their saries torn off, and very properly, yet the God-fearing hooligans had been taught that it was sinful to wear foreign cloth, and doubtless felt they were doing a religious act; can he not feel a little sympathy for thousands of women left with only rags, driven from home, for little children born of the flying mothers on roads in refuge camps? The misery is beyond description, Girl wives, pretty and sweet, with eyes half blind with weeping, distraught with terror; women who have seen their husbands hacked to pieces before their eye, in the way "Moplas consider as religious"; old women tottering, whose faces become written with anguish and who cry at a gentle touch and a kind look waking out of a stupor of misery only to weep, men who have lost all, hopeless, crushed, desperate, I have walked among thousands of them in the refuge camps, and some times heavy eyes would lift as a cloth was laid gently on the bare shoulder, and a faint watery smile of surprise would make the face even more piteous than the stupor. Eyes full of appeal, of agonised despair, of hopeless entreaty of helpless anguish, thousands of them camp after camp, "Shameful inhumanity proceeding in Malabar," says Mr. Gandhi. Shameful inhumanity indeed, wrought by the Moplas, and these are the victims, saved from extermination by British and Indian swords, For be it remembered the Moplas began the whole horrible business; the Government intervened to save their victims and these thousands have been saved. Mr. Gandhi would have hostilities suspended "—so that the Moplas may sweep down on the refugee camps, and finish their work?

I visited in Calicut three huge Committee camps, two Christian, and the Congress building and compound where doles of rice are given daily from, 7 A. M. to noon, In all, the arrangements were good. Big thatched sheds, and some buildings, shelter the women and children, the men sleep outside, They are all managed by Indians, the Zamorini's Committee distributing cloths and money to all, expect the Congress committee, which work independently and gives food from its own resource, At Palghat, similar arrangements are made by the Zamorini's Committee, and the order and care in feeding are good to see.

Let me finish with a beautiful story told to me Two Pulayas, the lowest of the submerged classes, were captured with others, and given the choice between Islam and Death. These, the outcaste of Hinduism, the untouchables, so loved the Hinduism which had been so unkind a step-mother to them, that they chose to die Hindus rather than to live Muslim. May the God of both, Muslim- and Hindus send His messengers to these heroic souls, and give them rebirth into the Faith for which they died. *New India, 29 November* 1921.

Wilful murders of Hindus and arson were first begun in my own place by Chembrasseri Thangal and his Lieutenant, another Thangal. You might have read accounts written by me in the Malabar journal which was sent to you last time. This contagion began to spread like wild fire and we began to hear of murders daily, Within a fortnight cold-blooded murders of Hindus became very common. From within the borders of Calicut and Ernad taluks refugees come in large numbers with tales of murders atrocities committed by the rebels. At Puthur Amson in Ernad only 12 miles northeast of Calicut—One day in broad daylight twenty-five persons who refused to embrace Islam were butchered and put into a well. One out of these who narrowly escaped death got out of the well when the rebels left the place and ran to Calicut for life. He is now in the hospital. So the accounts must be true as he himself was one of the victims.

During the last week news of numerous murders and forcible conversions came from another quarter also, Mannur near Aniyallur and Kadalundi railway station in Ernad taluk. This place also is only 14 miles away from Calicut. Every train to Calicut was carrying with it daily hundreds of refugees during the last week. If there were ten thousand refugees fed by the Relief Committee last week, it must have fed fifteen thousand this week. According to the statements given by them there must be at least fifty murders and numerous cases of conversions and house-burning. Can you conceive of a more ghastly and inhuman crime than the murders of babies and pregnant women? Two days back I had occasion to read a report given by a refugee in Calicut. A pregnant woman carrying 7 months was cut through the abdoman by a rebel and she was seen lying dead on the way with the dead child projecting out of the womb. How horrible! Another. a baby of six months was snatched away from the breast of his own mother and cut into two pieces. How heart-rending! Are these rebels human beings or monsters? From the same quarters numerous forcible conversions are also reported. One refugee has given statement that he had seen with his own eyes that the heads of a dozen people were being shaved by the rebels and afterwards they were asked to recite some passages from the *Quran*. This he witnessed from a tree. I wonder what is the authority of some people who contradict the news of murders, and forcible conversions of Hindus. Let them come here and test the veracity of these statements for themselves.

'Yesterday another report of murders came from a place very near Kottakal. The report says that eleven Hindus (males and females), were murdered by the rebels.

'A fortnight ago fifteen dead bodies of Hindus were seen under culvert on the road between Perinialmanna and Melatur.

"Will you not be sick of these stories of murders? All these reports are, as far as possible, proved also to be correct.

'Words fail to express my feelings of indignation and abhorrence which I experienced when I came to know of an instance of rape, committed by the rebels under Chembrasseri Thangal. A respectable Nayar Lady at Melatur was stripped naked by the rebels in the presence of her husband and brothers, who were made to stand close by with their hands tied behind When they shut their eyes in abhorrence they were compelled at the point of sword to open their eyes and witness the rape committed by the brute in their presence. I loathe even to write of such a mean action. I thank God that my family and relatives reached safe at Calicut without being dishonoured by these brutes, though we sustained serious loss of property and the loss of four lives (two servants and two relatives,—More afterwards). This instance of rape was communicated to me by one of her brothers confidentially. There are several instances of such mean atrocities which are not revealed by people. *New India 6th Dec. 1921.*

Truth is infinitely of more paramount importance than Hindu-Muslim unity or Swaraj, and therefore, we tell the Maulana Sahib and his co-religionists and India's revered leader Mahatma Gandhi —if he too is unaware of the events here--that atrocities committed by the Moplahs on the Hindus are unfortunately too true and that there is nothing in the deeds of Moplah rebels which a true non-violent non-co-operator can congratulate them for. What is it for which they deserve congratulation? Their wanton and unprovoked attack on the Hindus, the all but wholesale looting at their houses in Ernad, and parts of Valluvanad, Ponnani, and Calicut Taliques; the forcible conversion of Hindus in a few places in the beginning of the rebellion and the wholesale conversion of those who stick to their homes in its later stages, the brutal murder of inoffensive Hindus, men, women, and children in cold blood, without the slightest reason except that they are "Kaffirs" or belong to the same race as the Policemen, who insulted their Tangals or entered their Mosques, the desecration and burning of Hindu Temples the outrage on Hindu women and their forcible conversion and marriage by Moplahs; do these and similar atrocities proved beyond the shadow of a doubt by the statements recorded by us from the actual sufferers who have survived, deserve any congratulation? On the other hand should tthey not call forth the strongest condemnation from all right-minded men and more especially from a representative body of Mohamedans like the Khilafat Conference pledged to non-violence under all provocation? Did the Moplahs, who committed such atrocities, sacrifice their lives in the cause of their religion?

(Sd.) K. P. Kesahava Menon. Sec. Kerala Pro. Cong. Comit.	(Sd.) T. V. Mohamad. Sec. Ernad Khilafat Comit.
(Sd.) K. Madhavan Nair. Sec. Calicut Dis. Cong. Comit.	(Sd.) K. Karunakara Menon. Treas Karala Pro. Comit,

(Sd.) K. V. Gopal Menon.

Maulana Mohani justifies the looting of Hindus by Moplahs as lawful by way of commandeering in a war between the latter and the Government or as a matter of necessity when the Moplahs were forced to live in jungles. Maulana perhaps does not know that in the majority of cases, the almost wholesale looting of Hindu houses in portions of Ernad, Valluvanad and Ponani Taluques was perpetrated on the 21st, 22nd, and 23rd of August before the military had arrived in the affected area to arrest or fight the rebels even before Martial law had been declared. The Moplahs had not betaken themselves to jungles at the time as Moulana supposes nor had the Hindus as a class done anything to them to deserve their hostility. The out-break commenced on the 20th of August, the police and the District Magistrate withdrew from Tirunangadi to Calicut on the 21st and the policemen throughout the affected area had taken to their heels. There was no adversary to the Moplahs at the time whom the Hindus could possibly have helped or invited, and the attack on them was most wanton and unprovoked.

MADHAVAN NAIK.

APPENDIX IV

Proceedings of the conference at Calicut presided over by the Zamorin Maharaja.

VI. That the conference views with indignation and sorrow the attempts made in various quarters by interested parties to ignore or minimise the crimes commitied by the rebels such as

a. Brutally dishonouring women

b. Flaying people alive

c. Wholesale slaughter of men, women and children

d. Burning alive entire families

e. Forcibly converting people in thousands and slaying those who refused to get converted

f. Throwing half dead people into wells and leaving the victims for hours to struggle for escape till finally released from their sufferings by death.

g. Burning a great many and looting practically a Hindu and Christian houses in the disturbed area in which even Moplah women and children took part and robbing women of even the garments on their bodies, in short reducing the whole non-muslim population to abject destitution.

h. Cruelly insulting the religious sentiments of the Hindus by desecrating and destroying numerous temples in the disturbed area, killing cows within the temple precincts putting their entrails on the holy image and hanging the skulls on the walls and roofs.

APPENDIX V

Petition of Malabar Ladies to Lady Reading

To

HER GRACIOUS EXCELLENCY

THE COUNTESS OF READING,

Delhi.

The humble memorial of the bereaved and sorrow-stricken women of Malabar.

MAY IT PLEASE YOUR GRACIOUS AND

COMPASSIONATE LADYSHIP.

WE, the Hindu women of Malabar of varying ranks and stations in life who have recently been overwhelmed by the tremendous catastrophe known as the Moplah rebellion, take the liberty to supplicate your Ladyship for sympathy and succour.

2. Your Ladyship is doubtless aware that though our unhappy district has witnessed many Moplah outbreaks in the course of the last one hundred years, the present rebellion is unexampled in its magnitude as well as unprecedented in its ferocity. But it is possible that your Ladyship is not fully appraised of all the horrors and atrocities perpetrated by the fiendish rebels; of the many wells and tanks filled up with the mutilated, but often only half dead bodies of our nearest and dearest ones who refused to aban-

don the faith of our fathers; of pregnant women cut to pieces and left on the roadsides and in the jungles, with the unborn babe protruding from the mangled corpse; of our innocent and helpless children torn from our arms and done to death before our eyes and of our husbands and fathers tortured, flayed and burnt alive; of our hapless sisters forcibly carried away from the midst of kith and kin and subjected to every shame and outrage which the vile and brutal imagination of these inhuman hell-hounds could conceive of; of thousands of our homesteads reduced to cinder-mounds out of sheer savagery and a wanton spirit of destruction; of our places of worship desecrated and destroyed and of the images of the deity shamefully insulted by putting the entrails of slaughtered cows where flower garlands used to lie. or else smashed to pieces; of the wholesale looting of hard earned wealth of generations reducing many who were formerly rich and prosperous to publicly beg for a piece or two in the streets of Calicut, to buy salt or chilly or betel-leaf—rice being mercifully provided by the various relief agencies. These are not fables.

The wells full of rotting skeletons, the ruins which once were our dear homes, the heaps of stones which once were our places of worship—these are still here to attest to the truth. The cries of our murdered children in their death agonies are still ringing in our ears and will continue to haunt our memory till death brings us peace. We remember how driven out of our native hamlets we wandered starving and naked in the jungles and forests; we remember how we choked and stifled our babies' cries lest the sound should betray our hiding places to our relentless pursuers. We still vividly realise the moral and spiritual agony that thousand of us passed through when we were forcibly converted into the faith professed by these blood thirsty miscreants; we still have before us the sight of the unendurable and life long misery of those —fortunately few—of our most unhappy sisters who born and brought up in respectable families have been forcibly converted and then married to convict coolies. For five long months not a day has passed without its dread tale of horror to unfold.

3. Your gracious Ladyship's distracted memorialists have

endeavoured without exaggeration, without setting down aught in malice to convey at least some idea of the indescribably terrible agonies which they and thousands more of their sisters have been enduring for over five months now through this reign of inhuman frightfulness inaugurated and carried on in the name of the Khilafhat. We have briefly referred without going into their harrowing details to our heartrending tale of dishonour, outrage, rapine, and desolation. But if the past has been one of pain and anguish, the future is full of dread and gloom. We have to return to a ruined and desolated land. Our houses have been burnt or destroyed; may of our breadwinners killed; all our property looted; our cattle slaughtered. Repatriation without compensation means for us ruin, beggary, starvation. Will not the benign Government come to our aid and give us something to help us to begin life anew? We are now asked to settle down as paupers in the midst of the execrable fiends who robbed, insulted and murdered our loved ones—veritable demons such as hell itself could not let loose. Many of us shrink from the idea of going back to what there is left of our homes; for though the armed bands and rebels have been dispersed the rebellion cannot be said to be entirely quelled. It is like a venomous serpent whose spine has been partly broken, but whose poison fangs are still intact and whose striking power, if diminished, has not been destroyed. A few thousands of rebels have been killed and a few more thousands have been imprisoned, but as the Government are only too well aware many more thousands of rebels, looters, savagely militant evangelists and other inhuman monsters yet remain at large, a few in concealment, but most, moving about with arrogance openly threatening reprisals on all non-moslims who dare to return and resume possession of their property. Many refugees who went back have paid for their temerity with their lives. In fact, repatriation, if it is not to be a leap from the frying pan into the fire, must mean for the vast bulk of your Ladyship's impoverished and helpless memorialists and their families a hard inexorable problem of financial help, and adequate protection against renewed hellish outrages from which immunity would be utterly impossible as long as thousands of men and even women and children of this semi-savage and fanatical race in whom the worst instinct of earth hunger, blood-lust and rapine have been awakened to fierce activity are free to prey upon their peaceable and inoffensive neighbours who—let it be most respectfully emphasised—because of their implicit trust in the power and the will of a just and benign Government to protect them, had suffered their own art and capacity for selfdefence to emasculate and decay.

4. We, Your Ladyship's humble and sorrow-stricken memorialists do not seek vengeance. Our misery will not be rendered less by inflicting similar misery upon this barbarous and savage race; our dead will not return to us if their slayers are slaughtered. We would not be human, however, if we could ever forget the cruel and shameful outrages and indignities perpetrated upon us by a race to whom we have always endeavoured to be friendly and neigbourly: we would be hypocritical if, robbed of all our possessions we did not plead for some measure of compensation to help us out of the pauperism now forced upon us; we would be imbecile, if knowing the ungovernable, anti-social propensities and the deadly religious fanaticism of the moplah race we did not entreat the just and powerful government to protect the lives and honour of your humble sisters who have to live in the rebel-ravaged zone. Our ambition after all is low enough; sufficient compensation to save us and our children from starvation, and enough military protection against massacre and outrage are all that we want. We beseech Your Compassionate Ladyship to exercise all the benevolent influence that you possess with the government to see that our humble prayers are granted. But if the benign Government does not consider it possible to compensate us and to protect us in our native land we would most fervantly pray that free grants of land may be assigned to us in some neighbouring region which though less blessed with the lavish gifts of nature may also be less cursed by the cruelty and brutality of man.

We beg to remain,
Your Ladyship's most humble
and obedient servants,

APPENDIX VI

ON NON-CO-OPERATION

BY M. R. JAYAKAR

[We take the following extracts from the Presidential address of Mr. M. R. Jayakar at the Third Thana District Conference. Mr. Jayakar is a well-known Non-Co-operator who believes in the "principles and policy" of the movement and who joined the movement because he realised that "Our quarrel with the bureaucracy was far more substantial than our differences with the Congress Programme."]

The Failure of the Programme

The principles and the policy of the movement (N. C O.) are substantially sound and have achieved unexpected success. But, with every month that has passed, the need has been felt in many quarters of revising and adjusting the programme in the light of previous experience. When dispassionately judged by such experience it will be found that some details of the congress programme have not achieved the desired success on the contrary, they have formed weak links in the main. When these items were undertaken they evoked a large volume of adverse criticism in the ranks of Congress workers. Many of them have, no doubt, subordinated their differences, out of loyalty to the main cause, and quite a large number, out of their esteem and regard for the personality of the selfless and saintly promoter of the movement. But, notwithstanding this admirable display of loyalty among Congress men, the fact remains and has to be reckoned with, that many items have proved unsuccessful and perhaps act, in consequence as a clog on the movement. The soreness, which some of these details have caused, still remains and is operating to undivide some from others and makes them lukewarm or unwilling to throw their whole heart into this movement. If these co-workers of ours could be placated by a revision of the Congress programme, so that most of the earnest-minded workers for cause could substantially agree to its adoption, it would be a great advantage. And herein perhaps, lay the chief merit of the amendment moved by Mr. B. C. Pal, which was rejected by the majority at Calcutta. Taken at its highest, our success has not gone much beyond what that amendment would have made possible. It would have had the further advantage of retaining within our ranks many of our former associates, who are, at present, either lukewarm or hostile.

Experiment in youthful sacrifice

When once the necessity is recognized of revising the programme in the light of these comments, which are being made throughout the country, it will not be difficult to find out in what directions the programme has not achieved the expected success and the reasons for the same. For instance, the boycott of schools and colleges have not succeeded and even persons, of known and undoubted loyalty to the cause, complain that the action of Congress workers has caused more harm than good. They concentrated too much on the disruption of existing institutions and less on the creation and maintenance of new one on "national" lines. They forgot that a student cannot be left idle in the street and that, if the Congress must call him out, it can only be after it has provided for him a good substitute. In Bombay we let pass the psychological moment when we could have founded and reared up an excellent college with various branches. Public enthusiasm was ripe for it in the early part of the year, but we let it evaporate in declamation and emotional exaltation. Some went so far as to suggest that it was no part of the Congress programme to start national Colleges though the terms of the Congress Resolution specially provided for it. 50000 boys are out in idleness, says Sir Ashutosh Mukherji, some may glorify in this catastrophe, but there are many who regard this disruptive event with sad dismay. We have experimented too much in youthful sacrifice. Our youth have reciprocated with more live and tenderness than we have shown for their welfare The few good institutions which Congress workers have created, are suffering from our neglect and apathy and dragging a weary existence. The shadow of a name has, very often been pursued, to the abandonment of the substance, and we now find a large number of boys in the country, who are practically loafing in the streets, with a vague ambition "to do something patriotic",

The Lawyer-Failure

Our ban on lawyers has, likewise, not attained much success. Few lawyers, whose sacrifice of their practice has added strength to the Congress cause, have responded to the call. The prestige of British court in *civil* Suits between an *Indian and Indian* has not been destroyed and can not be so easily destroyed; for, ordinarily this variety of legal contests is not much colored with injustice, as political trials are. If lawyers had been called out, because, being a trained class of workers, the country wanted their undivided time and attention at this critical hour, it would have been a different matter, and, perhaps, if the call had been so made man, many more would have responded to it. But it was put the wrong way, and the lawyer was made to appear as if, in pursuing his profession, he was acting sinfully and must atone for it by a complete withdrawal from practice. The result was that, out of sheer self-respect, many really good lawyers have declined to respond to the call. Many could not give up their practice for pecuniary reasons and were too honestly adopt subterfuges calculated to create a semblance of sacrifice. Lawyers have become "pariahs" of our present political life. Some of them had borne the brunt of public agitation for more than two decades; their place is vacant and no class of workers of equal intelligence and keenness has come forward to take it.

A Foul Atmosphere

This part of the Congress programme has created a foul atmosphere of hypocrisy, intolerance, imposture and conceit in the Congress Camp, in which modesty, self-respect, and honesty often time find it hard to hold their place. In our enthusiasm, we forget that many lawyers value their profession for the training it affords in courage truthfulness, honor and toleration. No other profession trains a young man so well to withstand and expose injustice and to uphold the tradition of truth and honor. Our past political history of thirty-three years is a brilliant record of the services rendered by lawyers to the Congress cause. If a greater sacrifice than before was needed now on their part, a direct call on their self-respect and partriotism on this footing should have been made, but no good has arisen from putting the lawyer under the ban of ridicule and infamy. The call made upon them was singularly harsh. No other class of pubiic workers was required to give up his means of livelihood. The importing merchant support British prestige as much as, if not more than the lawyer and yet he stalks unabashed in the Congress camp without closing his shop. No ban was put on litigants, without whom the lawyer cannot thrive. I am therefore, surprised that notwithstanding so much hardship, so many lawyers have come out and are to be found in the vanguard of the movement. The few courts of justice, we called into existence have not had enough support and are a mockery.

Revise the Programme

The failure of these parts of the programme is now practically admitted and they are now pushed into the background. It would be better if, in revising the programme in the next Session of the Congress, these limps, which have ceased to function of respond to the laws of our growth, are boldly amputated. In any event, they make clear the necessity of a revision, so as to render the programme more effective, elastic and practical.

Enter the Councils

The fight requires to be carried on in manifold ways. Some may carry it in the Councils, face to face with the officials. Why cannot "Non-Co-operation," in its proper sense, be practised in the Councils? Sir P. M. Mehta, when he left the Council Hall with his colleagues on a memorable occasion or when he, face to face with the then home member, mercilessly unclocked the preposterous pretensions of the bureaucracy, was fighting with weapons and a spirit which many Non-Co-operators or the true and accredited brand may envy in these days If Non-Co-operation is an *attitude* of the mind, as its eminent author conceives it, and not so much a programme or a creed, a Council Hall is as fitting a place for its display as a mass meeting in a Marwadi Vidyalaya. The spirit resides in the mind and is independent of the environment. It is no ground to say that, often times, the environment frightens a weakling, for we do not build our doctrines only on the possibility of men being weak and timid.

N. C. O. Concession

We have already departed from the original rigor of our programme in this behalf. A Non-Co-operator can now compete at Municipal elections. He can offer advice to Government in or outside private interviews Non-co-operator papers do report the proceedings of the Legislative Bodies, comment on them, and suggest remedies for the benefit of the Government. Scarcely a non-Co-operator now-a-days speaks without referring to gubernatorial utterances and orders in Council. He comments on the policies of Government, suggesting remedies as he goes on with his comments. Several lawyers in Bombay, who are still in practice, are now allowed to occupy prominent places as speakers at Non-Co-operation meetings. This is as it should be, for we cannot afford to ignore or despise, in the stinted state as our resources, the co-operation of any honest workers, prepared to make a sacrifice commensurate with his capacity. This is all done now silently and as a concession. My plea is for making the programme so wide, elastic and natural, as to turn these concessions into acknowledged rights. The Congress Creed calls upon us to obtain Swaraj by all legitimate and peaceful means. All weapons all avenues of work and all manner of public workers are enjoined on us, for the attainment of the common end. Why set up ascetic standards, unpractical tests, and unnatural bans, which may often let in the dishonest but keep out the honest man, whose co-operation, even with a difference, is often worth loving. The programme may become theoretically less perfect, perhaps logically less consistent, but it will certainly be more natural, real and effective.

Suggested Modifications

The exact form of the modification must be left to future discussion. I would, therefore, suggest as follows:

(1) That foreign propaganda, so summarily put an end to at

the last Congress, be resumed and if possible extended within proper bounds. The Indian view has to be put forward before the civilised world. This is an urgent need of the hour. The Government are doing it from their own point of view, and we ought to do the same from ours.

(2) That the time limited be abandoned, for reasons mentioned in para 25 below.

(3) That the elections to Legislative Bodies, whenever a chance should occur, should be contested parhaps with the limitation, that in the Provinces, unless complete autonomy is introduced, Congressmen should not accept office under the present system of Government. This may be, if so desired, made conditional on Government agreeing to dissolve the present Bodies.

(4) A large modification of the educational boycott, including the total abrogation of the compulsory part of it. Attention should be concentrated more on the creation of national institutions than on the withdrawal of students as a set propaganda. When such institutions are projected, and some of them actually in existence, and they compete favorably with state aided institutions. I have no doubt that sufficient impulses have been generated in the country to secure the exercise of the option in favor of the former. Side by side with this, an intensive propaganda should be carried on in the Councils and outside, having for its object the popularisation of the Universities by a change of the Act governing them, and also the "nationalisation" of the existing system of state-aided education, so as to bring it into greater accord with the present-day requirements and aspirations of the people. To me, it seems to be such a pity that we have deserted this avenue of agitation, to be feebly utilised by a few persons in the present Councils, struggling against an unsuitable environment. Nine crores, which is nearly the total output on State education, we are not in a position to despise, and it seems wrong to wait for this reform till complete Swarajya is attained, which may or may not be for some time yet. Considerable harm has been done to the cause of education by the excinsion of this avenue work from the programme of Congress activities. The fate of primary

education in the Bombay presidency will clearly illustrate the point I am making.

(5) A large modification of the ban against lawyers, so as to admit of several grades of sacrifice from complete abstention from practice to a giving up of the entirety or a part of the earnings. A way should be found for getting as many lawyers as possible to work in this movement provided they are prepared to give the cause at least a part of their time or money. The Congress ought to modify its call, so as to make it possible for all honest-minded lawyers to bear the burden of the country's cause, commensurate with their capacity to sacrifice.

Similarly, in the matter of conducting defences in British courts, some curious departure have come to be made from the strict Congress rule. These departures only indicate that, in its operation, the rule has been found unpractical and irksome. Congressmen are not to engage pleaders nor offer a defence with legal aid. They are simply to make a " statement." A statement is as much an aid to the administration of justice as a lawyer—made defence, and in so far, it equally supports the prestige of British courts. Only, it has the disadvantage of being prolix and unconvincing. It, therefore, fails of its mark more often than a lawyer's defence.

Who can urge that the long and interesting statements made by the Ali Brothers and their co-accused, in the trial at Karachi were out of place? Yet they had all the features of a lawyer-made defence, as an aid to the court. The evidence was discussed, legal objections raised, relevancy commented on and the prosecution evidence answered. All this assistance was given to the court, helping it to arrive at truth and justice, precisely in the same way as a practising lawyer aids judicial administration.

If a statement is permitted, why cannot a lawyer be employed in Court to make it more convincing and exculpatory? A statement must be based on facts, and these facts become material only when proved. On what rational grounds can, therefore, a statement permitted and yet the material evidence supporting it disallowed? It is no answer to say that the statement is meant for the guidance of the *Swaraj* Courts when the same are established, for when that eventuality happens, a statement supported by evidence will be any a better help to these Swaraj Courts than a mere statement? It is obvious that no Swaraj. Court will liberate a man merely on his own statement, without further inquiry.

Civil Disobedience

We are on the eve of Mahatma Gandhi undertaking an important part of his programme by starting Civil Disobedience in a district in Surat. It is very difficult to offer any useful comment on this undertaking because beyond the general lines, his programme in its detail is not yet before the Country. We can only hope that the resistance to law will not be so undertaken as to be widely interpreted as a sort of charter for general lawlessness. That would be a catastrophe for which the country is not prepared. This seems also to be Mr. Gandhi's opinion, for he has very prudently circumscribed the practice of the resistance with very severe restrictions, involving a moral and economic preparation. To disobey specific orders of Government or their officials, which have no moral sanction behind them or are illegal in their inception, is a comparatively easy matter, fraught with no far-reaching harm to the community. The disobedience, in such a case commands the moral approval of the civilised community, and ends only by affecting the prestige of the promulgator of the order. But when a campaign is undertaken involving a wholesale and general defiance of order and authority, forces may arise, which, in the hands of inexperienced and enthusiastic associates or partisans, may reach extreme limits, involving the community in chaos, disorder and possibly violence. The country has had only a year's training in his (Mr. Gandhi) counsels of non-violent resistance—far too short a period for his countrymen to imbibe his spirit, in a manner worthy of his teaching. May we, therefore, hope that in launching on this undertaking he will seriously consider this aspect of the case? We shall of course, watch his experiment but with concern and solicitude, feeling secure in the hope, created by his magnificent personality, that in his hands the destinies of the country are perfectly safe.

APPENDIX VII

Extracts from the speech delivered by His Excellency Sir Harcourt Butler. Governor of the U. P. of Agra & Oudh at the opening of the U. P. Legislative Council,

Lucknow, 22nd January, 1921

Mr. President and Members of the Legislative Council, .

" Great efforts have been made to draw away young men from schools and colleges and to induce professional men to give up their careers. Great efforts have been made to prevent voters from going to the polls. But these efforts have met with little success. The elections have undoubtedly given the province a really representative legislative council. The chief opponents of the reforms have shown by word and act that their aim is not the ordered development of political institutions in India but the expulsions of Western civilization from India—a course involving the reversion to the condition of disorder, lawlessness and internecine strife such as prevailed in the unsettled times before the advent of British rule."

" The tenantry were widely stirred up. The criminal classes took advantage of the occasion and serious trouble ensued in which there was regrettable loss of life. A full report on the Rae Braeli disturbances will be published within a few days. It was fortunately possible to restore order without calling in military aid from outside, and for this I have already congratulated the local authorities and others concerned. Statements, I may say that all reports from both Rae Bareli and Fyzabad indicate that the tenantry are actuated by no hostility to Government or to Europeans. The agitators have endeavoured to stir up such hostility."

" As for my Government I have chosen as colleagues without

favour strong and independent men. They will have my complete confidence in all matters, and it is my desire that we should work together as far as possible as one Government. I shall endeavour to secure that we all, Europeans and Indians, work together on harmorious lines as brother-subjects of the King-Emperor ; and I pray that the Reforms Scheme which we are commencing to-day will and largely and effectively to the well-being and happiness of this ancient land of Hindustan."

APPENDIX VIII

Extracts from the speech delivered by His Excellency Sir Harcourt Butler at a meeting of the United Provinces Legislative Council

28th March 1921

Mr. President and Members of the Legislative Council,

" The recent disorder in Rae Bareli has necessitated a further reconsideration of the question. Whereas the former disorders in Rae Bareli were largely agrarian in origin the recent disorders were mainly political in origin and wholly revolutionary".

" The result of the disorders has been an unfortunate loss of life, for which the agitators are directly responsible, and a feeling of insecurity which if unchecked may spread with untoward results, affecting innocent and guilty alike. Confronted with an elemental question as to the maintenance of order, my Government came unanimously to the conclusion that it was necessary to stop the campaign of unconstitutional agitation and lying, *propaganda* which has been carried on the four south-eastern districts of Outh —Rae Bareli Partabgarh, Sultanpur and Fyzabad. We therefore applied to the Government of India to extend the Seditious Meetings Act to those four districts. This has been done".

" I believe that this action will have the support of this Council and of responsible people generally in this province. With the non-co-operators we can have nothing to do beyond meeting their mischievous activities. Their movement is a revolutionary movement playing on passion and pandering to ignorance but the mass of people are loyal and all their interests are bound up with the maintenance of order."

APPENDIX IX

Extracts from the speech by His Excellency Sir Harcourt Butler at a Dur ar held at Lucknow

17th December 1921

GENTLEMEN,

I am glad to have this opportunity of meeting you to-day, in formal assembly, and to outline to you the policy of the Government.

My Government was accused some months ago of being repressive. I have met that charge completely with facts and figures and proved that the Government has acted with due patience in spite of deliberate and repeated provocation. It has dealt with agitation under the ordinary law and has maintained order and security with reasonable success. Of late the agitators, whose openly avowed object is to make Government impossible, have entered on a campaign of increased activity Quite recently the Government received reports from several quarters foreshadowing lawlessness and disorder. The Collector of Meerut reported that civil disobedience had been openly preached at the District Congress at Garhmukhtesar, that cloth shops were picketted, that agitation was plainly on the increase, and that everything looked like working up to a climax at an early date. The Commissioner of Fyzabad reported that the situation was menacing in the Bara Banki district where the Deputy Commissioner could not appear without being hooted and the loyal section of population were frightened and disheartened. A speech was delivered in which the audience was asked by a political fanatic whether they would agree to murder the Deputy Commissioner and they replied with one voice that they would. The Commissioner also reported that things were menacing in the Tanda sub-division of the Fyzabad district. At Gonda regular volunteer corps had been instituted with officers From Cawnpore and Etawah reports came of a recrudescence of criminal intimidation. In Ballia the people were asked too prepare themselves for killing and being killed. Alarming reports were also received from Saharanpur, Aligarh and Gorakhpur.

Now all these reports reached the Government within three or four days. It was quite clear that we were on the verge of serious and widespread trouble. The Government decided, and decided unanimously, to apply the Criminal Law (Amendment) Act of 1908, part II, to the whole province at once and to issue instructions to Commissioners and District Officers to take all measures under the law necessary for the preservation of order and protection of loyal and peaceful citizens. This was followed by an open defiance to the Government signed by over seventy individuals in the *Independent* newspaper. As you are aware the ringleaders have been arrested. I do not propose to deal with individual cases; some of them are still under trial. I will only say this, that all the reports I have received from different parts of the province show that the action taken has had excellent result and has restored confidence to loyal and peaceful people. Indeed, there is a feeling of general relief. The Commissioner of Fyazabad reports "There has been a great improvement since I last wrote. The police who had resigned are now applying to be taken back." The Commissioner of Agra writes " The present Government policy appears to be generally welcomed." The Commissioner of Gorakhpur says " There is no doubt that the moderate party not only welcome the arrests but in some cases are jubilant over them." The Commissioner of Meerut reports that the action taken had " been hailed by all loyal persons with the greatest relief." He adds "our friends and the much harried police are in much better hearts and non-co-operator is no longer looked upon wtth dread by them." The Commissioner of Lucknow attributes the settling down of the Hindu population and especially the cultivating classes largely to the recent action of Government. A re-assuring report has come from Aligarh. The situation is still critical; but. I think. that it is well in hand, and I am convinced that if a policy of firmness is pursued and pursued steadily for some time we may reasonably hope to break the back of a conspiracy which openly avows its intention of trying to do away with Government and openly defies the law of the land.

Consider the position, gentlemen; What have the Congress and *Khilafat* movements done? *Satyagraha*, which Mr. Gandhi himself pronounced to be a " Himalayan blunder " ended in disgrace. The attempt to boycott colleges and schools failed signally. It did not affect in this province one per cent of the students and scholars. The attempt to boycott the law courts was wholly unsuccesful. The appeal to surrender titles given by and offices held under the Government fell on deaf ears. The efforts to seduce soldiers and policemen were almost in vain. But with each successive failure, they have sown wider the seeds of racial hatred and the spirit of lawlessness. The results cry out against them and their work. Their hands are dripping with innocent blood; and the cries of ruined homes and ravished women have gone up to heaven. This is the end of the idea of self-Government attained by non-violent revolution, an idea wholly fantastic and chimerical.

As is usual when Government takes vigorous action, there is a body of critics who have no experience or sense of government and who are frightened by action. They seem to think that law and order keep themselves. The truth is far otherwise. Law and order are mainly kept by force, and that with difficulty. They are very easily upset. You have had experience of disorder in southern Oudh, in which there was an orgy of violence, rape, rapine and arson. I do not hesitate to tell you that if the Government trifled with the present situation you would probably soon find your lives, your property and your honour in danger. The objection that action has been taken with warning is quite unfounded. More than once I have publicly declared that this Government would not tolerate disorder or intimidation. The aggressors are those who violate the law.

APPENDIX X

STATEMENT BY SIR L. PORTER

We have been vilified bitterly, every kind of abuse has been showered on us by non-co-operators, every form of insidious agitation has been tried, and we have stayed our hands.

Violent Agitators

I will mention the case of one of the men who has now been arrested and is undergoing imprisonment as a first-class misdemeanant. He made at least ten speeches up and down the country which our legal advisers informed us were clearly actionable I allude to Mr. Jawahir Lal Nehru. His final effort was a speech, somewhere in the west of the Province, in which he quoted word by word the sedition section, i. e, the promotion of disaffection against the Government as by law established and the section which deals with promoting hatred between classes of His Majesty's subjects, and he said that the object of his life was to carry out this promotion of sedition and disaffection. Still we did nothing. You may well ask why. We thought that the forces of reason and sobriety would re-establish their sway. We hoped that the great body of moderate opinion of the Provinces would be sufficiently powerful to assuage this movement and to stop the dissemination of poison, We were wrong. So far from losing any strength I do not hesitate to say that the movement has gone on gaining strength. Then came the time in November when we were confronted with reports from our trusted officers all over the provinces which left no doubt whatever in our minds that the situation had very greatly developed, and that there was imminent possibility (I would go further and say probability) of an outburst of violence in more than one district. I have here a big folio of reports. It is quite impossible for me in debate like this to quote them all. There are copies of reports from districts as wide apart and representative as Meerut. Cawnpur, Fyzabad, Etawah, Balia. Barabanki and the peaceful district of Aligarh, which, according to its member, Thakur Manak Singh, is now the scene of this campaign of repression. I should like, as a typical instance, to read out the description of the procedure which was adopted in the Barabanki district. The Barabanki district, as my friend on my right will bear me out, is a particularly difficult one. It is full of a class whom religious fanaticism particularly affects and when it once gets out of hand it is very difficult to deal with. I remember when I first came to India, there was tremendous outbreak of dacoity and violent crime in that and adjacent districts, which it took months to put down, at the cost of immense suffering to the population. This is one of the districts, which was selected as a focus in work on by these (what should I call them ?) advocates of soul force.

Soul Force

Their main activities were directed to stirring up religious fanaticism. In mosques, in bazars mendacious stories were told regarding the bombardment and desecration of the Sacred Places of Islam. They were told that Hindu and Mahomedan women had been outraged and that medicines issued from dispensaries were mixed with wine, and that the fat of cows and pigs was used in the manufacture of cloth. There was boycott and intimidation to prevent foreign cloth sellers from importing any more cloth, and to force them to sign a pledge not to do so. This went on until November and the beginning of December when the picketting of schools started. That is a typical report from a district which takes very little to set it ablaze. What has recently happened there you have already read in the papers. There are many other instances which strike me, but there is one typical instance from Etawah. There is a fair which has been held there for many years. It was picketted. People were prevented from coming in by open intimidation, and finally attempts were made to blacken the face of a Maulvi on his way to the Islamia High School, of which he is manager. I can multiply these instances, and, if any member of the Council wishes to know the representations which were received from these districts, I am perfectly willing to let him see the reports in order that he may satisfy himself as to what the real condition was.

Pandit Radha Kant Malviya: Will the Hon. Member read the report from Allahabad.

Sis Ludovic Porter: We had a report from the Commissioner of Allahabad. on whose judgment I place great reliance, just before we enforced this Act. He expressed his reasoned opinion that if we allowed matters to drift any further, there would be a widespread disaster. He also stated that from information he had received, the whole camp of non-co-operators, in Allahabad were particularly cheerful with regard to the outlook, and they thought great developments in their favour were shortly going to take place. Well that was our position. As to the nature of this non-violent non-co-operation, we had no delusions.

Criminal Intimidation

We know that criminal intimidation had been practised on the widest scale in many districts. I may say that the majority of districts where these associations existed, criminal intimidation of a subtle kind, namely to attack a man in his religious opinions or to attack him in his social relations, had been widely practised. We had an example here in Lucknow of ordinary intimidation. A member of the Council himself witnessed the unfortunate driver of an ekka being dragged off his ekka and beaten because he ventured to ply for hire on the 17th of November.

I know myself the case of a shop which was kept open for two or three days. The shopkeeper was surrounded by a howling mob, and he was told what would happen to him, if he did not shut up his shop. In Fatehpur they kept a blackboard, which was exhibited publicly, to show up the people, who ventured to buy foreign cloth. This is also a form of subtle and most cruel intimidation involving social boycott. You all know perfectly well the difficulties that exist in India in getting victims of this kind of tyranny to come forward and seek their legal redress in the ordinary courts of law. The difficulty of proving criminal intimidation is accentuated by the fact that it is not cognizable by the police. and, consequently the complainant has to go to court, but, owing to the difficulty of getting witnesses to prove his case, he usually compromises. Well that is the position which confronted us. There was a system of widespread intimidation. So far from the movement being on the verge of collapse, as certain optimists stated to-day, it was increasing in vigour. There was the usual lip service of non-violence, a profession which in me produces a feeling of nausea. Practice and precept, as we said in a letter to the Government of India, which they quoted in the debate "were poles as under." There were also, as my friend Kunwar Jagdish Parshad in his eloquent speech this morning has stated, constant endeavours to seduce Government servants from their duty. A great deal of pity has been showered on the non-co-operators by certain speakers to-day, but they never spared a moment to think what the police have gone through. Here in Lucknow Chauk, sub-inspectors and the rank and file of your own fellow countrymen have been grossly insulted, abused and their family life rendered intolerable. Are we not going to support them when such facts are brought to our notice? We are bound to support our loyal servants, who, through all these troubles, have served us faithfully. I am only asking for some recognition of the difficulty to which they are exposed in performing their duties, and in their daily life. With these facts before us we came to the conclusion —the Government as a whole came to the conclusion—that the Criminal Law Amendment should be extended to these Provinces. I think there can be no doubt that the whole Council are unanimous that law and order must be enforced. They may differ from us as to the method which we took,

The Arrests

I now come to the arrests which followed. The great majority of arrests were effected by the local authorities under the powers delegated to them. In one instance only so far as my memory serves, the Governor-in-Council issued orders for certain arrests, and that was for the leaders of Allahabad and Lucknow. What are the facts in regard to these particular arrests? These associations had been declared to be illegal. Immediately after their proclamation a manifesto was published on the 6th December with a pledge which was signed by 75 persons,

I will read the terms of that manifesto. "Having read and thoroughly understood the Government notification, etc., and knowing full well the consequences of not obeying them, we, etc , hereby pledge ourselves civilly to disobey without any objection all such Government orders and laws as may be determined from time to time by the Provincial Congress Committee, or by a committee appointed by or in this behalf. We further pledge ourselves to obey, in utter disregard of the consequences, all orders of the volunteer corps relating to such disobedience." Now gentlemen, what does that mean? It means that at the bidding of an irresponsible autocrat in Bombay, the members of this association pledged themselves blindly to disobey any law of the land. If that is not the essence of anarchy I do not know what is. We were told this morning in the very moderate speech of my friend Mr. Zafar Husain, that he did not think that this Act was enacted with a view to the present juncture. Of course it was not. Nobody could forsee this madness which has come over India during the last two years. It was enacted to meet an outbreak of anarchy in Bengal. Could there be anything worse than the present position, that a body of men numbering thousands, totally irresponsible, very many of them now of a dangerous character, (not at first, but they are steadily deteriorating) pledge themselves to disobey any law when they were asked to do so by a gentlemen in Bombay, for this is what this pledge means? How could any Government carry on, that would not accept that challenge? In consequence of this, we issued orders for the arrest and production of a certain number, not all, of the leaders. In doing so we have now the support and authority of the Government of India. The Government has informed us that they agree with us in holding that the persons who deliberately organise associations, avowedly intended to break the law, or associations the members of which are pledged blindly to disobey any laws, are liable to criminal prosecution. Following on that came the meeting at Allahabad, at which the Superintendent of Police, who had been deputed to execute a search warrant, was present. This meeting deliberately reaffirmed this pledge in his presence. Now, I think if we analyse the objections that have been taken to the prosecutions they very largely centre round those persons, the leaders and members of this meeting, who have been prosecuted and convicted. In all they number, I, think, something like 100. I have stated the facts, and I accept the responsibility. I see no other way out. As long as any Government exists they have to deal with men who offer a challenge like that, in the method in which we did.

APPENDIX XI

BARABANKI DISORDERS

Lucknow, 18th January

In a view of the various rumours that were current regarding the situation at Barabanki. * * *

A lengthy official communique has just now been issued based on the report of the Deputy Commissioner.

* * *

At the same time, with effect from the 23rd November 1921, the Criminal Law Amendment Act was applied to the Province. Its immediate effect was good, and several volunteers who had been parading in uniform doffed their sashes and were disbanded.

Khilafat Agitators

Unfortunately, however, Khilafat agitators, who had publicly announced in the press of the 18th November that Barabanki Tahsil was being prepared for civil disobedience by the end of November, considered this act a suitable one to infringe. They redoubled their efforts and collected considerable sums, mainly for the Angora Fund, both through members of the 46 Khilafat committees established in this district and by itinery volunteers, who were paid for their services, either by fixed monthly salaries or by a percentage on collections. Between the 19th and 24th December, four volunteers were arrested under Section 7 (1) and 17 (2) of the Act, and these arrests were reported to have had a temporary beneficial effect. By the 3rd January, when the District delegates returned from the Ahmedabad conference. the leaders decided to take action openly. On the 4th it was reported to me that large numbers of volunteers would march into the city under the command of their zemindar leaders. No precise information however, could be obtained as to their intentions. On the morning of the 7th January batches of volunteers began to issue chiefly from the Congress Office from which was hung a Khilafat flag and a large notice calling on people to enlist as volunteers. These volunteers were mostly from outside villages and were headed by petty zemindars. They were all Mahomedans and had been worked up to a high pitch of religious enthusiasm. Many of them had their Qurans slung round their necks. They had apparently been incited to a state bordering on religious frenzy by exhortations from their leaders, that their religion was being destroyed by the British Government. They were wild in their abuse of Government, officials and specially the Police. The whole religious street in front of the Congress office resounded with religious shouts and cries of " Victory to Islam ". The cry of " Allah ho Akbar " was uttered as a war cry with fanatical zeal, specially when any arrests were made.

The Arrests

I had deputed Mr. Colton, Superintendent of Police, and Babu Ambikanandan Singh, Sub-Divisional Officer to take up a position opposite the Congress office and to arrest the ring leaders and the most truculent of the volunteers as it did not appear to be safe to allow them to remain at large, specially as fresh volunteers continued to pour into the city. Those selected were marched down under an escort to the Jail. * * *

The procession was accompanied by noisy music and the usual shouts of non-co-operation were raised. He (Chaudhari Athar Ali) refused to go before the Deputy Magistrate as requested but mounting the steps of the Congress office delivered a speech. After reciting certain words from the Qoran he addressed the crowd, and in a loud voice, declared that this tyrannical Government or tyrannical race (both versions are given) should be destroyed. The crowd which was in a state of fanatical frenzy, replied, '*Amin*, it will be destroyed immediately ". He exhorted the crowd to " become volunteers, enrol volunteers and fill the jails—victory to Islam ". The cry was taken up by the crowd. Seeing that the speech was causing great excitement, the Deputy Magistrate directed the police to produce him before him. He refused to go to the jail in the *Ekka* provided by the Deputy Magistrate. but insisted on going on foot, taking a circuitous route at the head of the procession of 500 or 1,000 men. He stopped the procession at various places and at these halts the usual *jais* were raised. The police were abused and Government servants were called dogs and pigs. On this day ten volunteers were arrested. On this date also there was the same commotion in the city, but the number of volunteers decreased.

Throughout the four days the volunteers created disturbances. It was obvious that the movement was entirely a Mahomedan one Not a single Hindu volunteer appeared. The Mahomedan volunteers and the crowd which cheered them on were filled with religious enthusiasm and hatred of the British Government. The intention of their leaders apparently, was to provoke the Police to acts of violence against them, and also to prove that they could insult the Government official with impunity, and were not afraid to go to jail. The following remark made in jail by Nawab Ali, an ex-vakil, a few minutes after his sentence, in the presence of two magistrates and a large number of pleaders, is significant. " By imprisonment people would get accustomed to the horrors of jail. By shooting they would learn to bare their breasts to rifle shots and bayonets. Men ready to be shot should now be enlisted. " The accused have been convicted.—*The Pioneer January 20, 1922.*

APPENDIX XII

THE GORAKHPUR TRAGEDY

Gorakhpur, 7th February

From early morning on Saturday a large number of volunteers were noticed arriving at Chauri Chaura and collecting on the Gorakhpur side of the railway station. They then proceeded towards the Bhapa Bazar, and formed a procession. They said that they were going to picket the bazar, and they proceeded towards the bazar through the police station grounds, although this was not their direct route. The procession consisted roughly of 3,000 people, and was headed by four or five voluuteers in khaddar uniform. Some of them had swaraj flags in their hands. After the main body of the procession had gone on, there were a few stragglers with whom the police, it is alleged, had some interchange of remarks. It is also stated that one or two of the stragglers were hustled by some of the chowkidars.

The Mob breaks Loose

It is impossible to say exactly what happened next but at any rate the stragglers shouted out and main procession came back and started throwing kanker at the Police. For some time the attack was confined to vicious kanker throwing, in which thousands of volunteers were engaged. The sub-inspector, finding that the affair was taking a more serious turn, asked the rioters to desist, but they would not take any heed, and attacked the police with lathies. The sub-inspector, in order to frighten the mob, fired a few shots in the air. This infuriated the mob, who made a rush towards the thana with lathies and spears. A few policemen were knocked down, and the remainder of the police went inside the thana buildings for protection. One or two policemen must have fired on the mob in earnest, as some of the rioters had received gunshot wounds, but whether the firing took place before the rush or after it is not known yet. By this time several of the policemen had been killed outside the police buildings, and one party fetched oil and straw and set fire to the thana at various points. This drove the entire police force out of the buildings.

They were immediately set upon by the mob and done to death in the most brutal manner. Their heads were battered with hinges torn from the doors of the thana, and then the bodies were soaked in oil and burnt. The charred remains were recovered, some in front of the thana, others in the thana compound and one at the back of the thana. Some of the armed policemen had obviously been battered to death by their own muskets. There was a certain amount of money in the thana and it is suspected that the rioters, having killed the policemen, looted the thana and then set fire to the buildings. The sub-Inspector's family quarters, it is believed, were also looted, and cash and jewellery were removed, but the inmates were not interfered with. The family quarters also bear marks of violence. The windows have been removed, and there are wide apertures in the roof. After having completely destroyed the police station the rioters dismantled the railway line in two places, and cut the telegraph wires. They threatened to kill the railway station master and the post master of Chauri Chaura if they sent any messages to the authorities at Gorakhpur. In all 22 policemen, including two Sub Inspectors, one head constable, 15 constables, four chowkidars and a servant of the Sub-Inspector were killed. Among the dead were found two of the rioters. A constable, and a chowkidar, who were at the police station during the attack escaped, and these men have been traced, and it is believed that their statement will throw considerable light on the whole affair. Complete quiet has now been restored. The Commissioner, the Magistrate and the Superintendent of Police visited the scene immediately on receipt of information, and restored confidence among the village people and the railway and telegraph lines were quickly repaired. Mr. Sands, the Deputy Inspector General of Police, attended the funeral of the dead policemen. The authorities immediately after the incident, invited three prominent gentlemen of Gorakhpur, one of whom is a non-co-operator, to visit the scene of the tragedy. *The Pioneer February 9, 1922.*

APPENDIX XIII

BENGAL

His Excellency's Speech at the St. Andrew's Day Dinner, on 30th November 1920

GENTLEMEN,

Among other things non-co-operation is to achieve is swaraj in one year. Mr. Gandhi has said so himself. The question is—do the people of Bengal want this particular form of swaraj? Being a shrewd and intelligent people they will doubtless wish to satisfy themselves first of all as to what precisely this swaraj is. Fortunately we are able to answer that question with authority, because Mr. Gandhi had issued a very clear explanation of what he means by swaraj in a small manual entitled ' Indian Home Rule," a new edition of which was published by Messrs. Ganesh & Co., of Madras, last year. I earnestly commend a perusal of it to all who are interested in the future of the land we live in. * *

Very well, if this is the sort of thing that people want by all means let them adopt non-co-operation. But I do not believe for a moment that this is what people want. And that, no doubt, is why we find so many other reasons advanced for adopting non-co-operation. It is claimed for it for example, that it is a saintly weapon in the hands of an oppressed people engaged in a righteous struggle against a tyrannous and unrighteous Government. Let us examine its credentials so that we may see to what extent the claim to righteousness can be sustained. In its earliest phase, when it was known as *Satyagraha*, its result were admittedly evil. The Hunter Committee was unanimous in its opinion that its effect was to engender "a familiarity and sympathy with disobedience to laws" and " to undermine the law abiding instincts which stand between society and outbreaks of violence at a time when their full strength was required." And, indeed, Mr. Gandhi himself confessed himself sorry that when he embarked upon a mass movement " he under-rated the forces of evil, and that he was obliged to pause and consider how best to meet the situation." Then again another object of the non-co-operators is to re-impose Turkish Administration upon the non-Turkish peoples who have so long suffered under it. The fact that under Turkish administration calculated attempts have been made to exterminate the Armenian people—one of the most horrible chapters in the whole history of crime—is ignored, a matter for surprise, surely, in view of the innate abhorrence of violence professed by the originator of the movement. Indeed, any one making a comprehensive survey of the non-co-operation movement could scarcely be blamed if he came to the conclusion that the only password required to give admission to the non-co-operation camp was "race-hatred." And is Bengal going to tolerate a movement based upon hatred, and, therefore, rooted in evil? Surely the world has had its fill of hatred. Cast your eyes over the past six years, and what do you see? A world in agony. The peoples of this earth trailing their spectral way across a blood-soaked scene of destruction and desolation—a ghastly phantasmagoria of human suffering; a hideous calvary. Humanity in torment, scourged with sorrow, losing its hold upon hope, drifting derelict in a terrifying ocean of despair. That is what hatred has done for mankind. And is mankind going to tolerate those who would deliberately and of malice aforethought perpetuate this grisly tradition of hatred among men? Let us have the answer of the people of this country to that question. For myself I have faith in the better mind of the people of Bengal. Not for nothing did Job Charnock lay the foundations of this great city. The finger of destiny was even then tracing the future of Great Britain and India upon the rock of doom. For better or for worse our paths lie side by side. The policy of Great Britain has been fairly and frankly stated. We are inviting the people of India to co-operate with us in making and travelling over that road which will lead to an India fashioned in so far as its internal affairs are concerned in ever-increasing accordance with the genius of its peoples, and filling a position of ever increasing pride and honour in the great confederation of the British Empire. Can any one who has faith in the existence of an eternal and immutable principle of justice and right doubt what the final choice of the people of India will be? Surely not. And it is with an unshakeable faith in its future that I give you the toast of "The Land We Live in."

His Excellency's Speech at the St. Andrew's Dinner, on 30th November 1921

India to-day is honoured by another distinguished guest—the most distinguished, indeed save only one, whom the citizens of the British Empire could welcome, namely, the heir to the Empire's Throne—His Royal Highness the Prince of Wales. He has come with words of sympathy upon his lips and with feelings of affection in his heart for the "Land we live in." Can it be doubted, then that from all communities and all creeds he will receive a royal welcome? I confess that it was with amazement that I learned that there was a small section of people, in this land of all lands, who had so far forgotten the dictates of courtesy as to urge the boycott of the Royal visitor. The promoters of this movement claim, I believe, to represent the fine flower of the ancient culture and civilisation of India. Well one lives and learns. I had always been brought up to believe that courtesy towards a guest was a deep-rooted tradition with the Indian people. And so I still believe it to be, though there may be some who have forgotten it. I do not believe that this attitude represents the real mind of India. Indeed, I know that it does not—for it was an Indian gentleman whose patriotism is beyond all possible question, who said to me when he read of the proposal "now must we bow our heads in shame for in showing rudeness to a guest we have touched the lowest depths of national humiliation and degradation." That, I believe, represents the best and, indeed, the real mind of India, for in India it has always been realised that discourtesy injures those who are guilty of it rather than those against whom it is practised, for it lowers them in the eyes of all right thinking men and indeed is sooner or later found by the man who is guilty of it to be a wound gnawing at his own self-respect. * * *

Already long strides have been taken along the path towards the ultimate goal. Indian and European have come closer together

—mutual understanding and goodwill are springing up between them. How much more could be achieved in this direction were it not for the black cloud of anger and hatred which has been brought into being by the apostles of revolution. From my experience of the past 12 months I have no hesitation in saying that a wonderful new era would have dawned for India already, had it not been for the wild passions which have been let loose upon the land by those who have pinned their faith to revolution.

They call the Government "Satanic". Have they then a monopoly of righteousness? The wild lawlessness and bloodshed at Giridih, Malegaon, Alighar, Malabar, Bombay and many other places—do these things not savour of the work of Satan? These are, indeed, but the heralds of red revolution. Let them look deep into their hearts and ask themselves in all seriousness if the salvation of India lies along such lines. * * *

His Excellency replying to the deputation of the representation of the people in the mufassal, held in Government House Calcutta on 2nd July 1921, said :—

Let me, therefore, repeat what I said a year ago. The facts are these: The Turkish troops in the fort at Mecca, in their attempts to overcome the Arabs who had rallied round the Sheriff bombarded the mosque containing the Kaaba. One of the Turkrish shells actually struck the Kaaba, burned a hole in the holy carpet and killed nine persons who were kneeling in prayer. These are the facts. The outrage was committed by the Turks, and I solemnly and categorically affirm that the British had nothing whatsoever to do with it. This being so, can you or any one suggest any other motive for the propagation of such falsehoods except the desire to create hatred against the British? * * *

His Excellency's speech at the Legislative Council on 19th December 1921

GENTLEMEN,

I will not go further back than October last. At the beginning of that month a manifesto, signed by Mr. Gandhi and a large number of other prominent non-co-operators, laid it down that it was the duty of every Indian soldier and Civilian to sever his connection with Government. There followed two important developments—an intensive campaign to undermine the loyalty of the police and a rapid development in the activities of " volunteer " corps. Alongside of these two significant developments was to be observed a rapid increase in open lawlessness and defiance of constituted authority. There were breaches of the peace in Howrah and Calcutta which are within the recollection of all. But such episodes were not confined to Calcutta. All over the Presidency persons were moving, stirring up disaffection among the masses. This process was assisted by an intensive campain of highly inflammatory speeches which had been in progress for some months past. Between the beginning of June and the middle of November, I received reports of no less than 4,265 meetings held in different parts of the province. I could quote passages from these speeches which are so inflammatory, so violent in their abuse that they would shock the Council. I refrain from doing so for the sole reason that I do not want to excite feeling unnecessarily. But I can assure the Council that, addressed, as in nine cases out of ten these speeches have been, to audiences made up of the illiterate and emotional masses, they could have but one result, namely that of spreading broadcast feelings of hatred and disaffection and of goading the people to violence. And that, indeed, has already been the actual result. Assaults on Settlement Officers have taken place. Government servants have been threatened and boycotted. Now let me return to Calcutta; and I take the events of November 17th to illustrate the state of affairs which had been reached. The life of city was paralysed. Were the police provocative? Certainly not. On the contrary the almost universal complaint made to me was that the police remained inactive and refrained from making arrests.

* * *

I have now to inform the Council of the discovery on the night of December 8th of a number of sinister weapons concealed in an untenanted house in the heart of the town. The nature of these weapons left little doubt as to the sort of use to which they were intended to to be put—swords ingeniously concealed in the handles of umbrellas, daggers of a peculiarly vicious type, tulwars and jars of acid. Very well, then I would lay stress upon this—that with so many recent outbreaks of roiting in the streets of the city fresh in one's mind, and with these further evidences of the sort of activities which were in progress at the movement, it was not unreasonable as a precautionary measure to have recourse to a limited number of military patrols.'

Only three days ago an Urdu manuscript leaflet was found posted up in the city of which the following is a translation :—

" What are you thinking about only ? Just come face to face with your opponent. Let yourself be cut to pieces, even to death but do not let any loss come to the Khilafat. Do not look towards Bagdad, neither do you look towards the Army, but kill your enemy right and left. Do not let any of your enemy to be left unkilled if you see him, and do not think that you are alone, because you are being helped by Imam Mehdi, who is standing in front of you. Call him, just fly a flag in your hand and cry out Khoda, Khoda, beat a drum in the name of Din Muhammad throughout the lanes."

Governor's Warning

Calcutta, February 11

Speaking at the Trades Association dinner in Calcutta, Lord Ronaldshay, the Governor of Bengal, made a lengthy reference to the political outlook.

It would be the height of unwisdom, said His Excellency, to close one's eyes to the gravity of the situation with which not only the Government but society in the widest meaning of that term is now faced. It seems desirable to call attention to this because there still appear to be quite a number of people who in spite of all that has happened, in spite of the resort to violence which has characterised the Non-co-operation movement in Malabar, Malegaon, Giridih. Aligarh, Bombay and many other places have not yet grasped the seriousness or the nearness of the danger, whit which the country is threatened.

Take the case of the Non-co-operation volunteers. We are told by some that we ought to withdraw our notification under the Act of 1908 declaring these volunteer corps to be unlawful association. A recommendation to that effect has quite recently been made to the Government by the Legislative Council. It is true that under the existing constitution, we are still responsible to Parliament for the maintenance of law and order and though it would no doubt save us much trouble and anxiety if we were able to transfer the responsibility from our own shoulders to those of the Legislative Council, we cannot do so. Nevertheless I have always regarded it as my duty to consider with the utmost care any recommendations which the Council makes and in this case I am calling for special reports as to the nature and extent of the present activities of these volunteers in different parts of the province in order that I may have the fullest and most up-to-date information before me.

On the Defensive

In considering the matter in the meanwhile, I would point out to the public at large something which, judging by the criticism to which we are subjected, had been overlooked, namely, that from the very beginning of the Non-co-operation movement right up to the present time, the Government have been on the defensive. It is the Non-co-operators who have always attacked and by so doing have compelled the Government to take up weapons for its defence,

For example I have heard it suggested that the Government have goaded the Non-co-operators into Civil Disobedience by the measures which they have recently taken. Nothing could be further from the truth. The policy of civil disobedience was accepted by the All-India Congress Committee at the beginning of November and it was not until towards the end of that month that action against the volunteers was taken. Mr. Gandhi himself, in moving the civil disobedience resolution on November 4th defined civil disobedience as a civil revolution, which, wherever practised would mean the end of the Government's authority and open defiance of the Government and its laws.

Well, that seems to be explicit enough and it seems a little unreasonable, surely, that those who profess to be opposed to such a revolution, should seriously urge the Government to lay aside the weapons, which it has only taken up to protect itself against, to use Mr. Gandhi's words once more "the destruction of its authority and the open defiance of its laws.". Do those who object to these volunteer-corps being declared to be unlawful associations realise what these corps have been brought into existence for? They have no excuse for not knowing, because Mr. Gandhi has himself explained quite frankly the object, for which they are being recruited. He declared at the conference held in Bombay on January 14th that, even if a round table conference was to be held he would not stop the enlistment of volunteers for a single moment. Why, because the enlistment was a preparation for civil disobedience.

The Critics Answered

There can be no doubt on that point at all, for we have also the letter written by Pandit Kunzru to Mr. Jinnah, in which he states that Mr. Gandhi declared explicitly at the conference that the enrolment and training of volunteers for starting civil disobedience must be continued. Very well then, what we are asked to do is this: To declare that the volunteer corps enrolled and trained for civil disobedience are lawful associations. Do those who urge us to take this step regard civil disobedience as a lawful form of political activity? If they do not, by what process of reasoning, do they argue that the agency by which civil disobedience is to be carried out should be declared by Government to be a lawful agency?

Now let us consider for a moment what the Non-co-operators mean by civil disobedience in its most developed form. It has been explained by Mr. Dip Narayan Singh a leading Non-co-operator of Behar. The procedure is to be as follows;—The chief civil officer in the area selected for its operation is to be given seven days to hand over the district to the Non-co-operators. The residents in the area are then to be ordered to disobey all the orders and laws of the Government and to refuse to pay taxes, register documents, and so on. At the same time the police station and courts are to be surrounded and the officials to be told to deposit their uniforms and other badges of office. The police stations and courts will then be treated as Swaraj property.

You well see that this bears out to the full declaration made by Mr, Gandhi, in moving the civil disobedience resolution at the meeting of the All-India Congress Committee on November 4th, that his programme of civil disobedience constitutes a civil revolution, which, wherever practised, will mean the end of the Government's authority and the open defiance of Government and its laws. Again I would ask, to those who wish these volunteers to be declared to be lawful wish to see this programme put into operation without a resort to violence, which will drench the country in blood?

The Lesson of Chauri Chaura

Even the milder forms of Non-co-operation activity such as picketing,—which is often claimed by the Non-co-operators to be peaceful pastime though even this claim is no longer maintained by Mr. Gandhi as I shall show in a moment—result in wild orgies of violence as we have been painfully reminded again, within the last few days by the horrible crime at Chauri Chaura in the United Provinces. This outbreak, in which 21 police men and chaukidars were violently beaten to death was deliberately organised, we are told, in the report from the Commissioners, by the volunteers, and if picketing results in orgies of murder and destruction of this kind what are likely to be results of attempts to put into operation the full pledged programme of Civil Disobedience to which I have already referred?

But it seems, as I have already remarked that Mr. Gandhi no longer maintains that all picketing is peaceful, for writing in his newspaper, "Young India" a short time ago, he says that in connection with the proposal for a round table conference his suggestion was that all picketing, except bona-fide peaceful picketing should be suspended pending the result of the conference. Clearly then, in Mr. Gandhi's opinion picketing is of two kinds, bona fide peaceful picketing on the one hand, and picketing which is not bona fide and peaceful on the other. Very well then, Mr. Gandhi knows that picketing is not peaceful. He must know that the more drastic forms of civil disobedience, which he is now determined to embark upon, must lead to violence.

The Issue

Is it possible under these circumstances to come to any conclusion other than that reached by the Government of India, that the issue is no longer between this or that programme of political advance, but between lawiessness and all its dangerous consequences on the one hand, and on the other hand, the maintenance of those principles, which lie at the root of civilised Governments.

In Bengal civil disobedience has already taken the form in a number of districts of a refusal to pay the "chaukidari" tax, and I have already received complaints from landholders that tenants are refusing to pay their rent throughout the province.

A general spirit of contempt for authority and defiance of law and order is being fostered. Well, respect for lawful authority and a general willingness on the part of the people to observe the law are the pillars upon which the very existence of society rests. If these be cut away, society fall into the abyss of anarchy and is shattered. It is recorded of a famous figure in history that he fiddled while Rome was burning. The story is one which is not without its moral for the present day.

APPENDIX XV

Extracts from the speech of the Hon'ble Sir Henry Wheeler, Member in charge of Political Department

What is the situatien with which we are faced ? It is the outcome of a movement which, in pursuit of certain political aims, as resulted in every province in India in bloodshed, disorder and confusion. A concise picture of the all India situation is contained in the report of the committee which recently inquired into the working of certain laws at Simla, and from it I quote their conclusion !—

Taking into consideration all the evidence we have received and the points to which we have adverted' and bearing in mind the still prevailing economic discontent, we cannot dismiss as improbable the danger of sudden sectarian, agrarian or labour disorder on a large scale culminating in riots.

They give instances of what they call 34 notable cases of disorder which have occurred in India during the current year. That is, most briefly, the position in India as a whole.

Let me now give a few illustrations of the position in Bengal, with which we are more particularly concerned, for it is perhaps apt to be overlooked that the whole problem does not centre round Calcutta alone. There is outside this city this vast Presidency of 40 millions people, and the difficulties in the *mufussal* are just as acute as here. To cite an example—in the district of Rangpur we have lately had reported an organisation of volunteers under a district captain and four vice-captains, definitely named, supported by two subordinate officers in each thana and a regular budget and funds, which, in addition to the better known objects of the non-co-operation movement, had set before itself the following five aims .—

(1) The organisation of volunteers to be ready for civil disobedience ;

(2) the preparation of the people to abstain from payment of chaukidari and union board tax ;

(3) the preparation of the tenants to refrain from paying rents ;

(4) the preparation of the people to boycott the thana and the law courts ;

(5) to boycott higher grade police and other officers especially with regard to foodstuffs, and if as a result of this the Government start their own store and make local arrangements it is felt that it will be possible to place difficulties in the way of transport.

This last line has in fact been taken and the Collector had to improvise supplies of food to various thanas and registration office.

The Council will have noticed the use of the term "civil disobedience," and in two other districts—namely, Noakhali and Faridpur—we have had the usual phenomena of a little knot of men forming themselves into a committee and saying : " We will have civil disobedience." What is civil disobedience understood to mean? Lest it be thought that it is merely an abstract subject for discussion, say, in a newspaper article, let me refer to an interesting definition of the term which we have recently had from a neighbouring province. The president of a meeting there lately outlined civil disobedience in the following terms :—

A notice calling upon Government to grant Swaraj within seven days will first be served upon the chief civil officer present in the locality selected for civil disobedience. Subsequently the residents of the particular locality will be directed to disobey all orders and laws of Government and to refuse to pay taxes, register documents, etc. At the same time police stations and courts will be surrounded and the officials told to deposit their uniforms and other badges of office. Thereafter police-stations and courts will be treated as Swaraj property. That is a position which, I put in to the Council, can be summed up in one word, "anarchy." That is the civil disobedience which is being preached, and which, if we are to believe the three speeches which we have just heard, is a little excitement which, in the words of one speaker, can be disposed of by a " flick of a handkerchief."

Now, Sir, I could carry on these examples from the *mufassal* to Chittagon, which has been in a state of disturbance and agitation since April last, and to Howrah where disturbances have been intermittent throughout the year, culminating in firing in the streets and in the death of a policeman. But the chronicle is too long, and I pass to Calcutta, where the remarks of His Excellency have fortunately shortened my task. We are all aware that the incessent stream of inflammatory oratory and agitation in Calcutta culminated on the 17th November in a paralysis of the life of the city and I was even surprised, when refreshing my memory as to those events, to see how openly what was done was gloried in by the leaders of the non-co-operation movement as having been done by their orders and direction. They were good enough to define in their instructions who might go about the streets and who might not, I have seen the statement that by the kindness of the Congress and the Khilafat committees certain shops would be allowed to open at 12 noon. There has never been any attempt to conceal the fact that the town was at that time, in the view of the non-co-operators, subject to their orders—subject by the processes of intimidation with which we are well acquainted.

Now if that was the position—and I submit that this is a correct statement of the position—Government was obviously confronted with the question of what they were to do. Was this state of affairs to continue or was it to be checked? We were approached on all sides, in this Council and by such responsible bodies as the British Indian Association, to intervene and to restore some measure of law and order in a condition of things which was fast drifting to chaos. In these circumstances we took the measures of which the Council is well aware, namely, to declare certain associations to be illegal, to introduce the Seditious Meetings Act in one district and prohibit by order of the Commissioner of Police, meetings and processions in Calcutta. I put it to the Council that short of these measures it would not have been possible to comply with the urgent requests so reasonably made to us from so many quarters to intervene in the interests of decent administration. That is the issue which is before the Council. Is it or is it not a fact that on the 17th of last month the people of this city were disgusted with the state of affairs and the prevailing terrorism? Is it or is it not a fact that constant pressure was brought to bear on Government by all sections of the people to bring about a better state of affairs? Can it in truth be said that the action of Government in attempting to curtail the activities of the gentlemen to whom the excitement is due has gone beyond the necessity of the case? If so, what is the alternative which the Council would place before Government? Of that, however, we have heard singularly little, except from Babu Surendra Nath Mallik, who advises us to withdraw all our orders, release prisoners, reduce sentences and place on their trial the military and the police—a solution which, I trust, will not commend itself to the better sense of the Council. * * *

APPENDIX XVI

BEHAR AND ORISSA

The Speech of the Hon. Mr. Macpherson, Member of Government, at the meeting of the legislative Council Patna,

24th January 1922

Sir, I desire to intervene at this stage of the debate, because I think it is proper that the House should know what the facts of the situation are before they make speeches and commit themselves to views which I hope they will be prepared to change after they know what the facts of the situation really are. I must ask your indulgence, if I find that what I have to say on this important occasion will take me beyond the usual time limits.

This is not the first occasion on which the Government of Behar and Orissa have explained to the public their attitude towards the non-co-operation movement and their reasons for the action taken on the 10th December last, which forms the subject of this Resolution. As the council is well aware, His Excellency the Governor received, a few days after that date, an influential deputation of Council Members and explained to them under what circumstances Government had been forced in defence of the public safety to take action under the criminal Law Amendment Act. An account of that deputation was published in all the newspapers which are commonly read in this Province and I trust it has been carefully perused by all the members of Council. I shall be pardoned if, when I come to discuss the expediency of action taken by Government, I go over again the ground covered by the communique which was issued on that occasion.

What was the position with which the Local Government were faced in the beginning of that month ? During the past twelve months they have seen these associations growing in number and boldness, spreading unrest throughout the public life of the Province, poisoning and confusing the minds of simple people, interfering with liberty of action, and not infrequently having to resort to force in order to compel obedience to their mandates. I have here a long list of cases in which persuasion was supplemented by force, sometimes force of a very disgraceful kind but I will not worry the Council by citing instances. This Province was not alone in these experiences, the organization of a volunteer revolutionary army was proceeding apace in neighbouring provinces also. The danger was being gradually realized by the Government of India and by other Local Governments, and before the end of November action under the Criminal Law Amendment Act had been taken by the Governments of the Punjab, the United Provinces Delhi, Bengal, and Assam. The Government of Bihar and Orissa stayed their hand till further inaction would have been criminal folly. The two circumstances which brought matters to a head in this province were

1 the immediate imminence of the introduction of the civil disobedience movement, particularly in the Tirhut Division, and,
2 the intensive preparations which were being made to organize a hostile *hartal* in Patna City against the visit of His Royal Highness the Prince of Wales on the 22nd and 23rd December. I know that certain local non-co-operation leaders have denied that there was any intention to start the civil disobedience movement within the Province during the month of December or even up to the present date, and we have been told that the Patna *Hartal* was a spontaneous movement on the part of the citizens. I think the Council will not be deceived by either of these assurances. After all Government had to follow the evidence at their disposal. There is one well-known leader

of the local non-co-operation camp, called Mr. Dip Narayan Singh. At a meeting held at Bhagalpur on the 16th November this gentleman outlined the programme which the leaders intended to follow. According to him a notice calling upon Government to grant *Swaraj* within seven days would first be served upon the chief civil officer present in the locality selected for civil disobedience, subsequently the residents of the particular locality would be directed to disobey all orders and laws of Government and to refuse to pay taxes, register documents, etc. At the same time police stations and courts would be surrounded and the officials told to deposit their uniforms and other badges of offices. Thereafter police stations and courts would be treated as *Swaraj* property. On the top of this declaration of policy, the Local Government had information that the first experiment would be made with the Basantpur police station in the Chapra District. Now this has been denied by the Congress party but the intention was an open secret. I was told about it after our last session by a member of this Council, who shall be nameless, and apart from our police reports, we had it on the authority of the *Motherland* dated the the 26th November, that Chapra had been selected as the first object of attack. This is what the *Motherland* of November 29th, 1921, says. The heading is—

" Civil Disobedience in Behar."

And the message runs :—

" A meeting of the Provincial Congress Committee was held at Patna on Sunday last. 33 delegates were elected for the coming session of the Indian National Congress at Ahmadabad. It was also resolved upon to form a volunteer corps in pursuance of the resolution of the All India Working Committee. The matter of selecting a suitable area for preparing it for Civil Disobedience was referred to the Provincial Working Committee which met on Monday last and decided in favour of Chapra in preference to the claims of Katra Thana in the district of Muzaffarpur, which were backed up by Muhammad Shafi."

The *Motherland* is a local organ of the revolutionary party and the property of Mr, Mazharul Haqq, who is the one of the shining lights in that camp, and presumably is in the confidance of the party. We know also from the public press that the previous volunteer associations, our old friends, the 'Khilafat' the 'Congress' and the 'Swaraj' volunteers were to be replaced by a new organization to be called the "National Volunteers" and we knew from our own reports that the particular name to be affected by the new organization of non-violent volunteers in Behar was the *Qaumi Sebak Dal*. Perhaps members of this Council would like to know something about the organization of this Behar *Sebak Dal*. This is what we heard about its organization.

Each squad was to consist of 20 volunteers. 20 squads would make a company *Maha Dal*, in this there would be 400 volunteers. Each squad would be under an officer.

Over 20 assistants there would be a higher officer. What he would dictate all the four hundred volunteers would have to observe.

The Bihar *Sebak Dal's* duty would be "Revolution" even if they had to sacrifice their lives.

And this is what we were told about their plans of campaign :

It was first to attack all the police-stations of the district and to take them into their possession, after removing the Inspectors, Jamadars and the Police.

When the thana had been taken possession of, then the *Kachahri* would have to be taken possession of and the *Hakims* would be removed.

Civil disobedience would commence in Chapra District from village Basantpur, in Muzffarpur from thana Katra, and then Sitamarhi.

Such then was the information on which the Local Government had to act. Does the Council still wonder that action of the nature taken was taken? To those who protest that the information held by Government was unreliable I can only reply that it has been fully corroborated not only by what has happened in other Provinces and by published documents of the non-co-operation movement but also by what has happened under our very noses in this Province. The non-co-operators say that it was never in contemplation to make an attack on Basantpur police-station on the 10th December. We believe that this particular experiment was nipped to the bud by the Notification of the same date, which found the leaders assembled at Chapra and threw them into consternation. But how do they explain the raids which were actually made at a somewhat later date on the police-station of Sonbarsa, Raghupur and Mahua in the District of Muzffarpur, or the attempt to picket the Gaya Civil Courts on the opening day after the X'mas holidays, which was only frustrated by the despatch of troops from Patna to Gaya on the previous evening? Were all these fortuitous and accidental? Do all these evidences of intention exist only in the heated imagination of the police? I shall have occasion later to tell the Council what effect these raids have had on the internal condition of the Muzaffarpur District. My present object is only to prove that when the Local Government took action under the Criminal Law Amendment Act on the 10th December, they were fully justified in believing that the civil disobedience movement would be started at a very early date in the Tirhut Division.

I do not wish to weary the Council by going into details regarding the Patna *hartal*. It seemed to Government, and with good reason, that efforts were being made to impose an intolerable tyranny on the citizens of Patna at a time when the representatives of the people, who sit in this Council, had extended to his Royal Highness a most cordial welcome and had voted a special grant to make that welcome worthy of the occasion. The object of the non-co-operators was to substitute for the welcome the same kind of deliberate insult that had been attempted to be offered to the Royal visitor at Benares and Allahabad. Government, I say, would have been open to the gravest reproach if it had made no effort to counteract that mean and wicked project, which was so foreign to the innate bospitality and reverence of the Indian people, and particularly repugnant, one would imagine, to the sturdy loyalty of Bihar. Under this double compulsion then Government decided that the time had come to follow the example of its neighbours. Members of Council know as well as I do what followed. There was, as Government expected there would be, much excitement in the city—the stirring of a hornet, nest always has this sort of reaction.

Sir, let not this Conncil be deceived by any cry of repression, by any false appeal for the freedom of association and the freedom of speech. This Government is not out for repression. It has no desire to interfere with political activity or freedom of speech. When Mr. Gandhi and his friends use these phrases, what they mean is license to preach sedition, and liberty to foment rebellion and revolution. Let us see how the system works in practice I will read to the Council a recent report on condition of the Muzaffarpur District. It is dated the 5th January:—

"The Muzaffarpur District still continues to be in very disturbed state particularly the Sitamarhi Sub division, where it is reported that law and order are decreasing daily and Magistrates are even insulted in their own Courts. The Sitamarhi Sub-jail is said to be practically in a state of mutiny, the prisoners shouting and singing all day until about 10 P.M., while on one occasion a warder was rushed and knocked down. Additional police have been asked for this subdivision and are badly required. The Masses in this district are said to have no longer any dread of going to jail owing to the inducements held out to them that they will be treated as political prisoners and fare better than in their own homes. The police have come in for more than their fair share of attention from the non-co-operators during the week and the Superintendent of Police is of opinion that his force bas become exasperated almost beyond endurance by the gross insults and abuse that has been heaped upon them.

On the 26th December 1921, about 200 volunteers escorted by a large and noisy mob forced their way into the Sonbarsa Thana compound in the Sitamarhi Subdivision, carrying swaraj flag and repeating the Delhi fatwa The thana police were told that to remain in Government service was for a Hindu equivalent to eating cow's flesh and for a Muhammadan to eating pig. Later the crowd became more insulting and abusive and though seven of the ringleaders were arrested, the crowd did not disperse until nearly midnight. Following this incident the whole of the thana staff were boycotted, the services of the barber, washermen and even supplies of food were stopped, until the divisional inspector succeeded in intervening.

At Raghupur Police-station in the same district, 300 volunteers appeared and told the sub-inspector that on the 1st January they would plant the swaraj flag in the compound and take possession of the police-station. At Mahua Police-station, the Police were also grossly abused and insulted and similar reports have been received by the Superintendent of Police from other police stations in the district.

Mention was made in last week's report of a fracas in the Court compound at Hajipur where alms were being distributed to the poor. This was followed on the same day by a parade of 100 Sevak Dal volunteers in front of the Hajipur police-station who shouted *Sarkar ki nokri karna haram hai* and grossly abused the Police,

Reports received from factories also indicate a serious state of unrest in the Mufassal. Mr. G. P, Danby writing from Bowarrah factory mentions that noisy shouting bands of volunteers are moving about the country making themselves a general nuisance and that to all appearance mob law prevails. The Belsand Factory in this district is reported to have been surrounded on the 4th January by a large mob shouting *Gandhi ki jai.* Europeans and loyal Indians are expressing their disappointment that Government did not continue strong measures against the non-co-operation movement."

That is a police report, and lest the Council may think it is highly coloured I will read a shorter note of the Divisional Commissioner, Mr. Scroope, who is a man of sober judgment.

Mr, Mansfield, Subdivisional Officer Sitamarhi, came to see

me yesterday before I left for Bankipur. He is a level-headed officer and in no sense an alarmist. He informed me that the police are no longer able to deal with non-co-operators in Sitamarhi town. The latter are practically in possession of the liquor shops which they now picket with impunity. They also haunt the neighbourhood of the Court and create much noise and disorder during the trial to political cases. They ask to be arrested and some of them who have been placed under trial under section 290, Indian Penal Code have been grossly insulting to the Magistrate. The journeys to and from Court of persons under trial for a political offence are made regular occasions for noisy demonstrations and abuse of Government. Mr. Mansfield's considered opinion is that non-co-operators are now entirely out of hand, that the existing police force is quite unequal to the task of keeping them in check and that law and order have practically ceased to exist in Sitamarhi town.

The sub-jail can only be described as in a state of mutiny. It is much overcrowded containing about 90 inmates (I am not certain of the exact number ; almost all are under trials) and certain influential non-no-operators under trials have been preaching defiance and insubordination to their companions. The result is a total absence of discipline ; the undertrials sing and shout at the top of their voices throughout the day and most of the night and any attempts on the part of the warders to enforce order and obedience are wholly ignored.

Here is a latter report of the doings of one of these roving bands of whom mention is made in the police report. The Superintendent of Police writes on the 21st January.

At the same time I received a telegram from Mr. Gray, Meanchupra.

" All roads here stopped by volunteers. No carts or servants allowed works. Come if possible, position critical ".

I left at 2 P. M. and arrived Meanchupra at about 3 P. M.

About 500 yards on the road west of Meanchupra I found some volunteers sitting on a culvert guarding the road. On arrival at the Bungalow I found Mr. and Mrs. Gray and their three children absolutely shut off and isolated by three volunteers. All the Factory work had been stopped as the jamadar peons and coolies were not allowed to enter the factory so that there was no one to cut the sugarcane etc. All carts had been stopped, volunteers cutting the ropes of the bullocks and driving them away. Even the house servant had been stopped from going to the bungalow from their village. There was no bearer, cooks *mashalchi*, *dhobe*, garden coolies or even *murgiwala*. Mrs. Grey had to dig up the potatoes in the garden, cook the food, wash up the dishes, etc., and her ayah asked her (as well she might) if it was true that the British Raj was over.

Sir, these are the facts which have already compelled Government to post a force of additional police to the Sitamarhi subdivision, and I do not disguise from the Council that they may force us at no distant date to take even sterner measures to preserve the peace of the district, and of other districts that are similarly threatened. If Government find it necessary later to present to Council a bill of costs which will not be at all to their liking, let them thank their non-co-operation friends for the gift.

I know we shall be met with the old cry of repression, but in this case it is a stupid cry. No Government of this country wants repression for repression's sake, and least of all the Government of Bihar and Orissa, which includes within its number three distinguished Indians who have never been accused of any lack of political independance. For my own part I claim that no one welcomed more keenly than I did the inauguration of the new reforms era in India. I had the confident hope (and in this matter I speak also for my hon'ble colleague, Sir Havilland Le Mesurier) that we had before us a great and inspiring task of friendly co-operation with educated Indians, which would at no very distant date place this country in the forefront of the common-wealth of nations. Sir, this great task has for the moment been heavily handicapped and hampered by the poisonous cult of non-co-operation, a cult which has embittered and clouded the political life of India and caused discouragement to all the friends of reform. It has made life a burden and weariness to all ranks of Government officers. to the responsible agents of Government in districts and to the directing staff at headquarters but I have still hope that the better sense of India will prevail and that the clouds will clear away. It is to you, members of the Council, that Government look to give a lead to the public which you represent, in the fight against this great danger which menaces India. The danger is not one which threatens only the officers of Government, professional men, and men of wealth and property. The interests of the common people, the patient cultivators and the toiling workmen, are just as much at stake. It is they who will suffer most, if revolution comes, as the same classes are suffering to day in Russia where they are perishing in millions as a result of the disintegration of ordered Government. I call therefore upon the representatives of all classes in this assembly to consider what is their duty, their solemn duty, on this occasion. The choice is between the orderly progress of India towards a future of brightest promise and the perilous path of revolution which leads to darkness and death. There is no midway between them. I appeal to you, gentlemen of the Council, to put aside any pre-conceived notions or prepared speeches with which you may have entered this hall to-day and to look at the position in all its naked truth. The question you have to decide for yourself is whether you stand for orderly Government or revolution. I trust that the hon'ble mover himself will realize his responsibility in the light of these remarks and withdraw his resolution now that it has served its purpose of securing a full discussion of the political situation.

The following is taken from the speech delivered by the Hon. Mr. Hammond, the officiating Chief Secretary of the Bihar and Orissa Government, during the recent debate in the Provincial Council on the political situation. *The Pioneer 1st February, 22.*

APPENDIX XVII

Disgraceful Tyranny

Has the hon. member read what has just happened in Guntur, in Madras, where rents are being withheld? Is he aware that not in one but in two or three districts in the Province there have been refusals to pay chaukidari taxes: that we have read not one but several speeches advocating this refusal? May I tell the Council that barely three or four days ago, in the district of Puri, a Panch assessor was murdered while endeavouring to collect chaukidari tax? Swami Vidyanand and others who followed and desclaimed against repressive laws enquired what have the "volunteers' done? It is a pertinent question, and, with your permission, Sir, I will give a few instances by way of answer. Time does not allow me to go through all their nefarious activities, but if Hon. members want to know what the "volunteers" have done, apart from enforced *hartal* and the ordinary common forms of secret intimidation, ask the widow of the Mahomedan, Mazir Ali Kalal, whose corpse was exhumed in Ranchi, thrown upon the public road and the face beaten in with a brick; ask Gopi Khar at Chatra, who on the 3rd January was beaten and taken with his face blackened through the town because his wife committed the foul crime of selling food to those who visited liquor shops. Is that persuasion? Is this *Ahimsa?* ask the woman of Kateya, Mussammatt Paremia Koerin, near Siwan, who was stripped naked and driven through the village by a howling mob. She complained as well she might to the Government police officer, who, when he went to hold an enquiry was attacked by a mob—a demonstration in force of soul-force! A speaker later in the debate declaimed against those, the Planters and the police, whose courage, he said, took the form of delight in tyrannising over the poor and of oppressing their fellow-countrymen." I ask in all sincerity what are these cases I have related but a dis-graceful tyranny; are they not, indeed, opperession of the poor?' "What right?" I shall be asked 'have you to lay these crimes at the doors of the non-co-operation party?" The answer is, that when men publicly oppose the funeral it is not irrational to believe that thay are concerned with the subsequent exhumation of the corpse. In the other cases I have mentioned evidence has been taken and there is the judicial finding.

North and South of the Ganges

Another member asked me to explain the difference between the positions north and south of the Ganges. Let us take this town of Patna. The hon. member did not, as some do, deny *in toto* that, there had been intimidation. I say there is in fact but little difference. In Tirhut the crime manifest and overt, and in Patna it is suppressed. Have the Council heard of those poor beggars who received tickets entitling to go to Gulzarbagh on the morning of the 22nd December and get blankets? Do they know that these people were asked by "volunteers" on their way to show their tickets which were then taken and torn up, that the same day some of the beggars when returning from Gulzarbagh were deprived of the blankets which they had been given which were burnt, and the beggars had to be content with such warmth, as they could derive from the glow of enforced patriotism. The difference between this side of the Ganges and the other is that in Patna such things do not unfortunately in a large city attract much attention.

Oh! the shame of it, a blind beggar woman deprived of her blanket, but no violence of course was used, only soul-force. Babu Ganesh Dutt appealed to justice and sympathy. Do these beggers deserve no sympathy? Is there to be no justice done on their oppressors? I shall be told that the leaders of the movement disavow such action; that they deplore them as much as we do. Sir, we cannot separate the methods from the ideals of the revolutionary movement. I am prepared to believe that some of the leaders deplore violence and would try to restrain it, but I maintain, and I challenge, any hon. member here to disprove it that, conducted on the lines as it is, admitting such members as it does to its ranks, the non-co-operation movement must inevitably result in violence.

The Giridih Riots

Let us take the case to which reference had been made before in this Council, the serious riots which occurred at Giridih, and which ended in an attack upon the sub-jail and the thana and the burning of the records. From what did that originate? It is a simple story. A sold B a cow and said that she would yield 1½ seers of milk. B took the cow away and found that he did not get the guaranteed amount of milk. Lawyers here know that the law of warranty is a somewhat difficult and intricate matter. However the local self constituted Panches decided that, A should take back the cow and refund the money. He declined to do so; and then as sanction to enforce the orders of this local court applied that cruel engine of oppression, social, boycott. In all civilised communities the black-mailer is regarded with disgust and condemned. It has been for the non-co-operation party to use social blackmail as the basis of sanction to its ideals. The inevitable result of such a sanction is violence.

What are the "volunteers" doing? They are fishing in troubled waters. They tried—let us once again come back to Patna—to get the domestic servants to strike: they succeeded in persuading some of the motor-car drivers to desert their masters when their services were most required, What are the "volunteer's" doing? They are persuading raiyats to withhold rent. I know the case of a wealthy zamindar who had to borrow money from the bank to pay his Government revenue. I maintain, sir, that though honest men amongst the non-co-operators speak of non-violence the movement must inevitably lead to violence.

Take an instance from private life—let us again quote from Patna. A gentleman returning from Calcutta, a man well acquainted with the law of the land, found that his servant had, at the bidding of one gentleman who is an active recruiting officer of "volunteers," decided to break the contract made with his master. I have the best authority for saying this breach of contract resulted in righteous indignation which took the form of personal violence. What are these "volunteers" doing? They are provoking violence; they are picketting; they are intimidating; they are interfering between the master and servant, between landlord and tenant, between the railway and its employees.

"Volunteers" Recruited from Criminal Classes

I know it will be said that efforts have been made to purify the ranks. It was found, for example, in Chapra, that *doms*, registered as criminal tribes, were enlisted in the ranks of the national "volunteers." From the other districts, too, came reports of ex-convicts and persons of the "C" class register not only being enrolled but being welcomed. The efforts to remove these members and to purify the movement does not seem likely to be successful if we may judge from a leader's experience in the Bhagalpur Division, at Banka, in the district of Bhagalpur. There I am informed, when he visited some villages with a view to expelling the undesirables, he was himself expelled and told to mind his own business. I submit, sir, for the earnest consideration of this Council that you can not seperate principles from methods or the ideals from the agents who are employed. Lastly, we have had an appeal that this Council should share the responsibility for maintenance of law and order. We have been solemnly advised by some of the speakers that Government should abdicate from the duty imposed by Statute of maintaining law and order in favour of these "volunteers" who were, so we are asked to believe, inaugurated solely to prevent a recurrence of the scenes that occurred in Bombay—to stop women being stripped of their clothes in the streets, to stop murder and loot. Can Government for a moment, in view of the activities I have related, contemplate handing over the duty, the primary and essential duty of the police, to the Kanmi Sevak Dal? The question has only to be asked to show its absurdity.

The question of Counter-Propaganda

The only piece of practical advice we received from Mr. Madan was that propaganda should be met by counter propaganda. But there are difficulties.

First how many of the hon. members would be willing to take up the task of propaganda? Secondly, how many of them would be listened to if they did? How many of these would be able to obtain a hearing? I confess it seems-to me, when Hon. members have protested that Government do not publish all the facts, that the time may come when every district and Sub-Divisional Magistrate ought to be his own publicity officer. In the last week we should have had stories in the papers of ladies being insulted in Monghyr, pushed into the road, and spat upon. We should have read of the wife of a settlement Officer, with her sister-in-law, being insulted by school-boys one of the ladies having her head cut with a stone; and from many districts we should have heard that pitiful tale of little children whose lips can hardly lisp the popular war cry being taught to shout it, not as a tale of admiration for an ascetic idealist, nor as reverence for a person of mystic magnetism, but as a mark of racial hatred, a hymn of hate. We could have published instances from Muzaffarpur and Champaran of the insults to European's, of mob roaming about shouting and committing mischief. Hon. members would have heard of Magistrates unable to hold trials because of the noise in the Court compounds. All these and more should have been done in the way of counter propaganda, exposing the methods of what is in fact a revolutionary movement, but would much good have been done thereby? Is it not more important to take steps to prevent such things happening? I ask the hon. members to remember that every vote given in favour of this resolution is a direct encouragement to the non-co-operation party they profess to abhor.

APPENDIX XVIII

DEMAND FOR AN INDIAN "REPUBLIC"

Mr. Hazrat Mohani's Address

AHMEDABAD, DEC. 30—The following is the full text of the authorised translation of the address, which Moulana Hazrat Mohani delivered this afternoon and which was, from the beginning to the end a plea for the declaration from the lst January, 1922, of an Indian Republic called the United States of India to be attained by all possible and proper means, including guerilla warfare in case Martial Law was proclaimed.

GENTLEMEN—While thanking you for electing me to preside over this session of the All-India Muslim League I wish to say in all sincerity that the importance of this session of the League, in which the faith of Hindustan is to be decided required the choice of a person abler than myself, such as Moulana Muhammed Ali, Dr. Kitchlew or Moulana Abdul Kulam Azad to preside over its deliberation but, unfortunately, the Governmeut has forcibly taken away the first two gentlemen from us, I express my inability to accept the responsibility. Consequently, as the proverb goes, "if thou dos't not accept it willingly, it will be forced on thee" this great duty was placed on my weak shoulders. I wish to discharge it to the best of my ability. Success is in the hand of God.

The Aims of the League

The present condition of the League appears to be very weak, indeed, but this does not in the least derogate from its real importance for it was the All-India Muslim League which actually realised. The first and the most essential condition of Indian independence is the Hindu-Muslim unity, and now that it has been achieved it is the duty of the League to maintain it also. Besides, it is on the platform of the League that all sections of political opinion amongst the Musalmans, Extremists or Moderates, have so far been and in future will, probably, be brought together. Before going into the causes of the weakness of the League, it will be better to enumerate the aims and object of the League. These are (1) the attainment of Swaraj by the people of India by all peaceful and legitimate means; (2) to protect and advance the political, religious and other rights and interests of the Indian Musalmans; (3) to promote friendship and union between the Musalmans and other communities of India and (4) to maintain and strengthen brotherly relations between the Musalmans of India and those of other countries.

The League an old Calendar

The first of these is also known to be the creed of the Congress. Therefore, so long as the word Swaraj is not defined in consonance with Muslim desire and the means for its attainment are not amplified, it is only natural that Muslim interests in League should be clear. The third object, Hindu-Muslim unity, is the common object both of the League and the Congress. The fourth object, the unity of Muslim word, which has been, along with other questions, connected with the Khilafat has been specially taken up by the Khilafat Committee. There remains only the second object that is the protection of the special interest of the Muslmans. As to this, so long as a much greater and more important object, that is, the attainment of Swaraj still remains unachieved, people would rather direct their united efforts against the common enemy that look after their special interests. They will be attended to when the time comes for it. As if these causes were not sufficient in themselves, to decrease Muslim influence in the League, its rules and regulations were, unfortunately, so framed that, while public opinion has developed at a rapid pace most members of the League have not moved an inch from their first position. As a result, the League remains nothing more than an old calender. It is very necessary to remove the causes of the weakness of the League and to remove them immediately, for in proportion as we approach nearer and nearer to the goal of Swaraj the need of the League will be felt more and more, because questions of special Muslim rights will rise again with greater importance when India is free.

An Indian "Republic"

Our first duty, therefore, should be to reduce the fee for the membership of the League and thus increase its members, who will choose their representatives of the League every year. The members to the Council of the Provincial and the All-India Muslim Leagues should be chosen as in the case of the Congress every year. But the most pressing necessity of all is a change in the first object of the League to suit the changed Muslim conditions. Everyone of us knows that the word Swaraj has been definitely left vague and undefined in the creed of the Congress. The object of it has been that, if the Khilafat and the Panjab wrongs, are settled on the lines of our demands, then Swaraj within the British Empire will be considered sufficient; otherwise efforts will be directed towards the attainment of complete independence. But, gentlemen from the Muslim point of view it is not enough that we should stand for complete independence alone. It is necessary to decide upon the form that it should take and in my opinion it can only be an Indian Republic or on the lines of the United States of India.

Besides this, the term "peaceful", which defines and restricts the scope of the legitimate means for the attainment of Swaraj in the Congress creed, is opposed to the nature and religious aspirations of the Musalmans. Therefore, in the creed of the League the words "possible" and "Proper" should be substituted for the words "Legitimate" and "Peaceful". I will explain the matter in detail. The Musalmans should understand clearly that they derive a two-fold advantage from the establishment of an Indian Republic, firstly, the general benefit which they will undoubtedly share along with their Indian brethren as citizens of a common State and secondly, the special advantage which the Musalmans will derive from it is that, with every decline in the prestige and power of the British Empire, which, to-day is the worst enemy of Muslim countries, the Muslim world will get breathing time and opportunity to improve its conditions. Gentlemen, in spite of the present Hindu-Muslim unity, there still exists many serious misunderstandings and suspicions between these two great communities of Hindustan, and it is of primary importance that we should grasp the true nature of these misunderstandings. The Hindus have a lurking suspicion that given an opportunity, the Musalmans will either invite their co-religionists from outsite to invade India or will, at least help them in case they invaded to plunder and devastate Hindustan, and these misunderstandings are so deep-rooted and widespread that, so far as my knowledge goes, no Indian statesman has escaped in, except the late Lokamanya Tilak. On the other hand, the Musalmans suspect that on the achievement of Self-Government, the Hindus will acquire greater political powers and will use their numerical superiority to crush the Musalmans. Gentlemen, it is quite clear that these misunderstandings can only be won over by a compromise discussion and mutual and intimate knowledge, and it is an essential condition of this mutual understanding that the third party should not come between them.

Hindus and Muslims

The generality of Musalmans, with few exceptions, are afraid of the numerical superiority of the Hindus and are absolutely opposed to an ordinary reform scheme as a substitute for complete independence. The primary reason for this is that in a merely reformed, as contrasted with anindependent Government they will be under a double suspicion, first, a subjection to the Government of India, which will be common to Hindus and Musalmans, secondly, a rejection by a Hindu majority, which they will have to face in every department of the Government. On the other hand, if the danger of the English power is removed, the Musalmans will only have the Hindu Majority to fear. Fortunately this fear is such as will be automatically removed, with the establishment of the Indian republic for, while the Musalmans, as a whole, are in a minority in India, yet Nature has provided a compensation, for the Musalmans are not in a minority in all Provinces. In some Provinces, such as Kashmere, the Punjab, Sind, Bengal and Assam, the Musalmans are more numerous than the Hindus. This Muslim majority will be an assurance that in the United States of India the Hindu majority in Madras, Bombay and the United Provinces will not be allowed to overstep the limits of moderation against the Musalmans. Similarly, so long as a completely liberated India does not come into the hands of the Hindus and Musalmans themselves, the Hindus will be always suspicious that, in case of a foreign invasion. the Musalmans will aid their co-religionist invaders, but on the establishment of the Indian Republic, which will be shared in common by the Musalmans and Hindus there will be no possibility of such a suspicion, for no Musalman will desire that the power of even a Muslim foreigner should be established over this country.

The Mopla Rebellion

Gentlemen, I have just stated it as a necessary condition of the Hindu-Muslim compromise that the third party, the English, should not be allowed to step in between us. Otherwise, all our affairs will fall into disorder. Its best example is before you in the shape of the Mopla incident. You are probably aware that Hindu India has an open and direct complaint against the Moplas and an indirect complaint against all of us that the Moplas are plundering and spoiling their innocent Hindu neighbours, but probably, you are not aware that the Moplas justify their action on the ground that at such a critical juncture, when they are engaged in a war against the English, their neighbours not only do not help them or observe neutrality, but aid and assist the English in every possible way. They can, no doubt, contend that, while they are fighting a defensive war for the sake of their religion and have left their houses, property and belongings and taken refuge in hills and jungles, it is unfair to characterise as plunder their commandeering of money, provisions and other necessaries for their troops from the English or their supporters. Gentlemen, both are right in their complaints, but so far as my investigation goes, the cause of this mutual recrimination can be traced to the interference of the third party. It happens thus, whenever any English detachment suddenly appears in the locality and kills or captures the Moplas inhabitants of the place, rumour somehow spreads in the neighbourhood that the Hindu inhabitants of the place had invited the English army for their protection, with the result that after the departure of the English troops the Moplas of their neighbours do not hesitate to retaliate and consider the money and other belongings of the Hindus as lawful spoils of war taken from those who have aided and abetted the enemy. Were no such events have occurred, the Moplas and Hindus even now live peacefully side by side, Moplas do not commit any excesses against the Hindus, while the Hindus do not hesitate in helplng the Moplas to the best of their ability.

A National Parliament.

I have wandered far from my purpose, I meant to emphasise that, in the first clause dealing with the aims and objects of the League, the word "Swaraj" should be defined as complete republic. Otherwise, there is a danger that in the presence of a third party, Self-Government within the British Empire, instead of being beneficial, might actually prove injurious. The second amendment necessary is that the methods for the attainment of Swaraj should be amplified. In the place "peaceful" and 'legitimate" means "possible" and "proper" should be permitted. Thus, on the one hand, the opportunity of joining the League will be given to those who do not honestly believe Non-Co-operation alone as the sole path of salvation, recognising the possibility of other methods and adopting them also. On the other hand, the amendment will remove the complaint of those who believe the Non-Co-operation can under, no circumstances, remain peaceful to the last, and while subscribing to the creed of the Congress and, the first clause of the section dealing with the object of the League as a matter of policy and expediency, refuse to admit it as a faith for all times and circumstances or to remain non-violent even in intention.

Gentlemen, there are only two possible means of replacing one Government by another one, the destruction of the Government by sword and the establishment of another in its place, a method which has been followed in the world thus far. The second alternative is to sever all connection with the present Government, and to set up a better or organised Government; parallel to it and improve and develope it till the old order is dissolved and the new takes its place. Friends, to achieve this object, we must immediately set upon a separate and permanent foundation our courts, schools, arts, industries, army, police and a national parliament, Non-violent Non-Co-operation can only help to paralyse the Government, but cannot maintain it. The question now is, can such a parallel Government be established only through non-violent non-Co-operation of course, provided the rival Government does not interfere with its establishment, a condition which is obviously impossible. The rival Government will certainly interfere. We might contend that we will proceed on without work silently and quietly and in spite of goyernmental interference as is being done at present. A stage will, however, be reached ultimately when action on peaceful lines will absolutely become impossible, and then we will be forced to admit that a parallel Government can be started, but not continue to the last through peaceful means.

Governmental Policy

The example of Governmental repression is before your eyes. First, it attempted through Karachi trials to prevent the Musalmans from openly proclaiming the articles of their faith, when the people, undaunted by this decision of the Government, preached through the length and breadth of India that it was unlawful to serve in the army. The Government slowly overlooked those activities fearing lest a mere repetition of the Karachi resolution might lead to disaffection in the Army, and in order to divert the attention of the people from those activities, it suddenly, but deliberately declared the enrollment as unlawful. That might get an opportunity of striking at the Non-Co-operators. Like the moths that gather to sacrifice their lives round lighted candle, the advocates of civil disobedience swarmed to break this declaration of Lord Reading and cheerfully went in their thousands to goal. This is undoubtedly an example of self-sacrifice and self-effacement which will rightly move Mahatma Gandhi to ecstasy, but we detect another truth hidden in this demonstration of happiness and joy. It reveals to our eyes the last stage of both the repression of the Government and the patience of the people. The people are, no doubt, prepared to bear and suffer gladly the hardships of a few days of imprisonment but on the declaration of Martial Law the non-violent Non-Co-operation movement will prove totally insufficient and useless. Amongst the Musalmans, at least there will hardly be found a man who will be prepared to sacrifice his life uselessly. A man can only have one of the two feelings in his heart, when faced by the barrel of a gun, either to seek refuge in flight or to take advantage of the law of seif-preservation and despatch adversary to hell. The third alternative of cheerfully yielding up one's life to the enemy and considering it to be the one real success will remain confined to Mahatma Gandhi and some of his adherents and fellow thinkers. I, on my part, feart hat in general the reply to the Martial Law will be what is commonly called guerilla warfare, or in the words of the Quran "kill them wherever you find them." The responsibility lies with the representatives of the Musalmans. The members of the All-India Muslim League, should consider it their duty either to refrain from adopting No-Co-operation as their creed or free it from the limitation of keeping it, either by violence or non-violence, for it is not in our power to keep Non-Co-operation peaceful or otherwise. So long as the Government confines to the use of chains and fetters, Non-Co-operation can remain peaceful as it ist o-day, but if things go further and the Government has recourse to gallows or machine guns it will be impossible for the movement to remain non-violent.

Duty of Muslims

At this stage, some people would like to ask how is it that, while the Hindus are content to adopt non-violent non-Co-operation as the means for attaining independence, that the Musalmans are anxious to go a step further. The answer is that the liberation of Hindustan is as much a political duty of Musalmans as that of a Hindu. Owing to the question of Khilafat it has become a Musalmans religious duty also.

In this connection I should like to say just one word. The glories of Ghazhi Mustapah Kemal Pasha and the conclusion of the recent Franco—Turkish Treaty might create an idea in some people's minds that the evacuation of Smyrna by the Greeks is certain, and the restoration of Thrace to the Turks if not certain is within the bounds of possibility. Consequently they might entertain the hope that the struggle in the Near East is coming to a close. I want to warn all such people that the claims of the Musalmans of India are founded more on religious than political principles. So long as the Jazirat-ul-Arab (including Palsetine and Mesopotamia) are not absolutely freed from non-Muslim influence, and so long as the 'political and military power of the Khilafat is not fully restored the Musalmans of India cannot suspend their activities and efforts.

The Muslim Demands

The Muslim demands as regards the Khilafat are these :—(1) that in the pursuance of the promise of Mr. Lloyd George, Thrace and Shayrna, aiong with the city of Smyrn, should remain purely under Turkish control, so that the political status of the Khilafat Musalman, which is essential for the Khilafat should suffer no diminution, (2) all non-Turkish control should be removed from Constantinople, the shores of Marmora and the Dardanelles in order that the Khilafat at Constantinople may not be under non-Muslim control, which is essential for the Khilafat; (3) all naval and military restrictions imposed on the Khilafa should be removed, as otherwise, he would have no power to enforce the orders of the Khilafa; (4) the Jazirat-ul-Arab, including the Hedjaz, Palestine, and Mesopotamia, should be free from all non Muslim influence and not be under the British mandate, as it was the death-bed injunction of the prophet. It should be noted that in the fourth demand we wish the English to give up their mandate of Mesopotamia and Palestine and remove their influence from the Hedjaz. As to the question whether the Arabs will acknowledge the Sheriff of Mecca or the Sultan of Turkey as their Khilafa, or whether the Arab Government of Hedjaz, Mespotamia and Palestine will be independant or under the suzerainty of the Khilafa, they will be decided by the Musalmans. We do not want non-Muslim advice and assistance.

A Compact Between Congress and League

In my opinion, gentlemen, the most pressing necessity of Hindustan is the immediate conclusion of a definite compact between the Congress and the League. The Congress should not enter into any negotiations with the Government concerning Swaraj (1) until the minimum Muslim demands with regard the Khilafat are satisfied; (2) on the other hand, the Muslim should definitely bind themselves that even though their demands with regard to the Khilafat are satisfied, they, the Musalmans of India, will stand to the last by the side of their Hindu brethern for the attainment and preservation of Indian independence. Such a compact is necessary for the work because there are signs of the enemies of Indian independence, and we have to confess with regret that a number of deceitful Indians working with the foreigners are concentrating all their efforts to wreck the Hindu Muslim unity and create distrust and misunderstanding between the two communities. On the one hand, the Musalmans are being enticed by false hopes with regard to the Khilafat question. On the other some show toys of political concessions are being prepared as a gift for the Hindus even before the stipulated period of ten years. It is intended that in simplicity, the Musalmans should consider the return of Smyrna, etc, as the satisfaction their Khilafat demands, and slacken their efforts for the attainment of Swaraj, while the Hindus should be misled into believing a further instalment of reforms as the Swaraj itself, or at least, its precursor and begin to consider the Khilafat as an irrelevant question. There can be only one solution for all these problems. Hindus and Musalmans after mutual consultation, should have Indian independence declared by Mahatma Gandhi, and that in future neither the English might have an opportunity of deceiving nor India of being deceived. After the declaration of independence, the Congress and the League will have only one object left; that is preservation of Swaraj. The 1st January, 1922, is the best date for the purpose because we would thus have fulfilled the promise that we made to attain Swaraj within this year, and the people of India will achieve success in the eyes of God and man.

APPENDIX XIX

GOVERNMENT REPLIES.

Mr. Gandhi's Misstatements.

" Mass civil disobedience is fraught with such danger to the State that it must be met with sternness and severity."

So says the Government of India (Home Department) in the communique published below in reply to Mr. Gandhi's manifesto offering a postponement of civil disobedience on certain conditions which Government regard as impossible.

The Government statement makes it clear that the issue is between lawlessness and the maintenance of civilised government.

The manifesto issued by Mr. Gandhi on the 4th February justifying his determination to resort to mass civil disobedience contains a series of misstatements. Some of these are so important that the Government of India cannot allow them to pass unchallenged. In the first place they emphatically repudiate the statement that they have embarked on a policy of lawless repression and also the suggestion that the present campaign of civil disobedience has been forced on the non-co-operation party, in order to secure the elementary rights of free association, free speech and of a free press. The Government of India desire to draw attention to the fact that the decision to adopt a programme of civil disobodience was finally accepted on the 4th November, before the recent notification relating either to the Seditious Meetings Act or the Criminal Law Amendment Act, to whioh Mr. Gandhi unmistakeably refers were issued. It was in consequence of serious acts of lawlessness, committed by persons who professed to be followers of Mr. Gandhi and the non-co-operation movement, that the Government were forced to take measures, which are in strict accordance with the law for the protection of peaceful citizens in the pursuit of their lawful avocations.

A new and dangerous situation

2. Since the inauguration of the non-co-operation movement the Government of India actuated by a desire to avoid anything in the nature of the repression of political activity, even though it was of an extreme character, have restricted their action in relation thereto to such measures as were necessary for the maintenance of law and order and the preservation of public tranquility. Up to November no steps, save in Delhi last year, were taken against the volunteer associations. In November, however, the Government were confronted with a new and dangerous situation. In the course of the past year, there had been systematic attempts to tamper with the loyalty of the soldiers and the police, and there had occurred numerous outbreaks of serious disorders, directly attributable to the propaganda of the non-co-operation party amongst the ignorant and excitable masses. These outbreaks had resulted in grave loss of life, the growth of a dangerous spirit of lawlessness, and increasing disregard for lawful authority. In November they culminated in the grave riots in Bombay, in which 53 persons lost their lives and approximately 400 were wounded. On the same date dangerous manifestations of lawlessness occurred in many other places, and at this period it became clear that many of the volunteer associations had embarked on a systematic campaign of violence, intimidation and obstruction, to combat which proceedings under the Penal Code and the Code of Criminal procedure had proved ineffective.

More drastic Measures

In these circumstances the Government were reluctantly compelled to resort to measures of a more comprehensive and drastic character. Neverthleess, the operation of the Seditious Meetings Act was strictly limited to a few districts in which the risk of grave disturbance of the peace was specially great, and the application of the Criminal Law Amendment Act of 1908 was confined to associations, the majority of the members of which had habitually indulged in violence and intimidation. It is impossible here to set out in detail the evidence which justified the adoption of these measures in the different provinces. Abundant proof is. however, to be found in the published proceedings of the various legislative bodies, in the *Communiques* of the different local Governments, and in the pronouncements of the heads of the provinces. While resolute in their determination to enforce respect for law and order and to protect loyal and peaceful subjects of the Crown, the Government have at the same time taken every precaution possible to mitigate where desirable the conditions of imprisonment and to avoid any action which might have the appearance of vindictive severity. Ample proof of this will be found in the orders issued by the local Governments. Numerous offenders have been released, sentences have been reduced and special consideration has been shown in the case of persons convicted of offences under the Seditious Meeting's Act or the Cirminal Law Amendment Act. There is thus no shadow of justification for the charge that their policy has been one of indiscriminate and lawless repression.

A statement disproved

A further charge, which has been brought to Mr. Gandhi is that the recent measures of Government have involved a departure from the civilised policy laid down by His Excellency at the time of the apology of the Ali brothers, namely, that the Government of India should not interfere with the activities of the non-co-operators so long as they remained non-violent in word and deed. The following citation from the *communique* of Government of India issued on the 30th May, conclusively disproves this statement :—

" After explaining that in view of the solemn undertaking contained in the statement over their signature it had been decided to refrain from instituting criminal proceedings against Messrs. Mahammad Ali and Shaukat Ali, the Government of India observed, it must not be inferred from the original determination of the Government to prosecute for speeches inciting to violence that promoting disaffection of a less violent character is not an offence against the law. The Government of India desire to make it plain that they will enforce the law relating to offences against the

State, as and when they may think fit against any persons who have committed breaches of it."

The proposed conference

It remains for the Government of India to deal with the allegation that His Excellency summarily rejected the proposal for a conference, although the terms put forward by the conference at Bombay and accepted by the Working Committee of the Congress were quite in keeping with His Excellency's own requirements as indicated in his speech at Calcutta. How far this is from being the case will manifest from a comparison of his Excellency's speech with the terms proposed by the conference. His Excellency in that speech insisted on the imperative necessity, as a fundamental condition precedent to the discussion of any question of a conference of the discontinuance, of the unlawful activities of the non-co-operation party. No assurance on this point, was, however contained in proposals advanced by the conference. On the contrary, whilst the Government were asked to make concessions which not only included the withdrawal of the notifications under the Criminal Law Amendment and Seditious Meetings Acts and the release of persons convicted thereunder but also this release of persons convicted of offences designed to affect the loyalty of the army; and the submission to an arbitration committee of the cases of other persons convicted under the ordinary law of the land, there was no suggestion that any of the illegal activities of the non-co-operators other than hartals, picquetting and civil disobedience should cease. Moreover, it was evident from the statements made by Mr. Gandhi at the conferenee, that he intended to continue the enrolment of volunteers in prohibital associations and preparations for civil disobedience. Further, Mr. Gandhi made also it is apparent that the proposed round table conference would be called merely to register his decrees. It is idle to suggest that terms of this character fulfilled in any way the essentials laid down by His Excellency or can reasonably be described as having been made in response to the sentiments expressed by him.

Impossible Requests.

Finally, the Government of Indin desire to draw attention to the demands put forward in the concluding para of Mr. Gandhi's present manifesto, which exceeded even the demands made by the Working Committee of the Congress. Mr. Gandhi's demands now include: (1) the release of all prisoners convicted or under trial for non-violent activities; (2) a guarantee that Government will refrain absolutely from interference with all non-violent activities of the non-co-operation party, even though they fall within the purview of the Indian Penal Code, or in other words an undertaking that Government will indefinitely hold in abeyance in regard to the non-co-operators the ordinary and long established law of the land. In return for these concessions he indicated that he intends to continue the illegal and seditious propaganda and operation of the non-co-operation party and merely appears to postpone civil disobedience of an aggressive character until the offenders now in jail have had an opportunity of reviewing the whole situation. In the same paragraph he re-affirms the unalterable character of the demands of his party. The Government of India are confident that all right thinking citizens will recognise that this manifesto constitutes no response whatever to the speech of His Excellency at Calcutta and that the demands made are such as no Government could discuss, much less accept.

Issue—Law versus lawlessness

The alternatives that now confront the people of India are such as sophistry can no longer obscure or disguise. The issue is no longer between this or that programme of political advance, but between lawlessness with all its dangerous consequences on the one hand, and on the other the maintenance of those principles which lie at the root of all civilised Government. Mass civil disobedience is fraught with such danger to the State, that it must be met with sternness and severity. The Government entertain no doubt that in any measures which they may have to take for its suppression, they can count on the support and assistance of all law-abiding and loyal citizens of His Majesty.

APPENDIX XX

N. C. O. RESOLUTION

Ahmedabad, December 28.

The following was put by Mahatma Gandhi. " Whereas since the holding of the last National Congress, the people of India have found from actual experience that by reason of the adoption of non-violent non-co-operation the country has made great advance in fearlessness, self-sacrifice and self-respect, and whereas the movement has greatly damaged the prestige of the Government, and, whereas, on the whole the country is rapidly progressing towards Swaraj, this Congress confirms the resolution adopted at the Special session of the Congress at Calcutta and reaffirmed at Nagpur, and places on record the fixed determination of the Congress to continue the programme of non-violent Non-co-operation with greater vigour than hitherto, in such manner as each province may determine, till the Punjab and the Khilafat wrongs are redressed and Swaraj is established, and the control of the Government of India passed into the hands of the people, from that of an irresponsible corporation, and whereas the reason of the threat uttered by his Excellency the Viceroy in recent speeches and the consequent repression started by the Government of India, in the provinces by way of disbandment of Volunteer corps and forcible prohibition of public and even committee meetings in an illegal and high handed manner, and by the arrests of many Congress workers in several provinces, and wehreas this repression is manifestly intended to stifle all Congress and Khilafat activities and deprive the public of their assistance, this Congress resolves that all activities of the Congress be suspended, as far as necssary, and appeals to all quietly and without any demonstration to offer themselves for arrest by belonging to the Volunteer organisations to be formed throughout the country in terms of the resolution of the Working Committee, arrived at in Bombay, on the 23rd day of November last, provided that no one shall be accepted as Volunteer who does not sign the following pledge:—

The Pledge

"With God as witness, I solemnly declare that (1) I wish to be a member of the National Volunteer Corps; (2) So long as I remain a member of the Corps, I shall remain non-violent in word and deed, and shall earnestly endeavour to be non-violent in intent, since I believe that as India is circumstanced non-violence can help the Khilafat and the Punjab and result in the attainment of Swaraj and consolidation of unity among all the races and communities of India, whether Hindu, Mussalman, Sikh, Parsi Christian or Jew; (3) I believe in and shall endeavour always to promote such unity; (4) I believe in Swadeshi as essential for India's economic, political and moral salvation, and shall use handspun and hand-woven Khaddar to the exclusion of every other cloth, (5) as a Hindu, I believe in the justice and necessity of removing the evil of untouchability and shall on all possible occasions seek personal contact with, and endeavour to render service to, the submerged classes; (6) I shall carry out the instructions of my superior officers and all the regulations not inconsistent with the spirit of this pledge prescribed by the Volunteer Boards or the Working Committee or any other agency established by the Congress; (7) I am prepared to suffer imprisonment, assault, or even death for the sake of my religion, and my country, without resentment; (8) in the event of my imprisonment, I shall not claim from the Congress any support for my family or dependants.'

Volunteer corps

"This Congress trusts that every person of the age of 18 and over will immediately join the Volunteer organisations. Notwithstanding the proclamation prohibiting public meetings, and inasmuch as even Committee meetings have been attempted to be construed as public meetings, this Congress advises the holding of Committee meeting in enclosed places and by tickets and by previous announcements, at which as far as possible only speakers previously announced shall deliver written speeches, care being taken, in every case, to avoid the risk of provocation and possible violence by the public in consequence.

"This Congress is further of opinion that Civil Disobedience is the only civilized and effective substitute for an armed rebellion, whenever every other remedy for preventing arbitrary, tyrannical and emasculating use of authority by individuals or corporations, has been tried and, therefore, advises all Congress workers and others who believe in peaceful methods and are convinced that there is no remedy save some kind of sacrifice to dislodge the existing Government from its position of perfect irresponsibility to the people of India, to organise individual Civil Disobedience, and massed, when the mass of people have been sufficiently trained in the methods of non-violence, and otherwise in terms of the resolution therein of the last meeting of the All-India Congress Committee held at Delhi, this Congress is of opinion that in order to concentrate its attention upon Civil Disobedience, whether mass or individual (whether of an offensive or defensive character) under proper safeguards, and under instructions to be issued from time to time by the Working Committee or Provincial Congress Committee concerned, all other Congress activities should be suspended whenever and wherever, and to the extent to which it may be found necessary.

Mahatma the dictator

"This Congress calls upon all students of the age of 18 and over, particularly those studying in the national institutions and the staff thereof, immediately to sign the foregoing pledge and become members ef National Volunteer Corps.

In view of the impending arrest of a large number of Congress workers, this Congress, whilst requiring the ordinary machinery to remain intact and to be utlilised in the ordinary manner whenever feasible, hereby appoints until further instructions Mahatma Gandhi as the sole Executive authority of the Congress and invests him with the full powers of the All-India Congress Committee including the power to convene a special session of the Congress or of the All-India Congress Committee or the Working Committee, and also with power to appoint a successor in emergency.

"This Congress hereby confers upon the said successor and all subsequent successors appointed in turn by their predecessors, all this aforesaid power provided that nothing in this resolution shall be deemed to authorise Mahatma Gandhi or any of the aforesaid successors to conclude any terms of peace with the Government of India or the British Government without the previous sanction of the All-India Congress Committee to be finally ratified by the Congress specially convened for the purpose, (and provided also that the present Creed of the Congress shall in no case be altered by Mahatma Gandhi or his successors except with the leave of the Congress first obtained).

"This Congress congratulates all those patriots who are now undergoing imprisonment for the sake of their conscience or country, and realises that their sacrifice has considerably hastened the advent of Swaraj."

APPENDIX XXI

Mr. M. K. Gandhi's Statement

Before reading his written statement Mr. Gandhi spoke a few words as introductory remarks to the whole statement. He said: Before I read this statement, I would like to state that I entirely endorse the learned Advocate-General's remarks in connection with my humble self. I think that he was entirely fair to me in all the statements that he has made, because it is very true and I have no desire whatsoever to conceal from this Court the fact that to preach disaffection towards the existing system of Government has become almost a passion with me. And the learned Advocate-General is also entirely in the right when he says that my preaching of disaffection did not commence with my connection with "Young India" but that it commenced much earlier and in the statement that I am about to read it will be my painful duty to admit before this Court that it commenced much earlier than the period stated by the Advocate-General. It is the most painful duty with me but I have to discharge that duty knowing the responsibility that rested upon my shoulders.

And I wish to endorse all the blame that the Advocate-General has thrown on my shoulders in connection with the Bombay occurrence, Madras occurrences, and the Chouri Choura occurrences thinking over these things deeply, and sleeping over them night after night and examining my heart I have come to the conclusion that it is impossible for me to dissociate myself from the diabolical crimes of Chouri Choura or the mad outrages of Bombay. He is quite right when he says that as a man of responsibility, a man having received a fair share of education, having had a fair share of experience of this world, I should know the consequences of every one of my acts. I knew them. I knew that I was playing with fire. I ran the risk and if I was set free I would still do the same. I would be failing in my duty if I do not do so. I have felt it this morning that I would have failed in my duty if I did not say all what I said here just now. I wanted to avoid violence. Non-violence is the first article of my faith. It is the last article of my faith. But I had to make my choice. I had either to submit to a system which I considered has done an irreparable harm to my country or incur the risk of the mad fury of my people bursting forth when they understood the truth from my lips. I know that my people have sometimes gone mad. I am deeply sorry for it; and I am, therefore, here to submit not to a light penalty but to the highest penalty. I do not ask for mercy. I do not plead any extenuating act. I am here, therefore, to invite and submit to the highest penalty that can be inflicted upon me for what in law is a deliberate crime and what appears to me to be the highest duty of a citizen. The only course open to you, Mr. Judge, is, as I am just going to say in my statement,, either to resign your post or inflict on me the severest penalty if you believe that the system and law you are assisting to administer are good for the people. I do not expect that kind of conversion. But by the time I have finished with my statement you will, perhaps, have a glimpse of what is raging within my breast to run this maddest risk which a sane man can run.

WRITTEN STATEMENT

I owe it perhaps to the Indian public and to the public in England to placate which this prosecution is mainly taken up that I should explain why from a staunch loyalist and co-operator I have become an uncompromising disaffectionist and non-co-operator. To the court too I should say why I plead guilty to the charge of promoting disaffection towards the Government established by law in India.

My public life began in 1893 in South Africa in troubled weather. My first contact with British authority in that country was not of a happy character. I discovered that as a man and an Indian I had no rights. On the contrary I discovered that I had no rights as a man because I was an Indian.

But I was not baffled. I thought that this treatment of Indians was an excrescence upon a system that was intrinsically and mainly good. I gave the Government my voluntary and hearty co-operation, criticising it fully where I felt it was faulty but never wishing its destruction.

Consequently when the existence of the Empire was threatened in 1899 by the Boer challenge, I offered my services to it, raised a volunteer ambulance corps and served at several actions that took place for the relief of Ladysmith. Similarly in 1906 at the time of the Zulu revolt I raised a stretcher-bearer party and served till the end of the 'rebellion'. On both these occasions I received medals and was even mentioned in despatches. For my work in South Africa I was given by Lord Hardinge a Kaiser-i-Hind Gold Medal. When the war broke out in 1914 between England and Germany I raised a volunteer ambulance corps in London consisting of the then resident Indians in London, chiefly students. Its work was acknowledged by the authorities to be valuable. Lastly in India when a special appeal was made at the War Conference in Delhi in 1917 by Lord Chelmsford for recruits, I struggled at the cost of my health to raise a corps in

Kheda and the response was being made when the hostilities ceased and orders were received that no more recruits were wanted. In all these efforts at service I was actuated by the belief that was possible by such services to gain a status of full equality in the Empire for my countrymen.

The first shock came in the shape of the Rowlatt Act a law designed to rob the people of all real freedom. I felt called upon to lead an intensive agitation against it. Then followed the Punjab horrors beginning with the massacre at Jallianwala Bagh and culminating in crawling orders, public floggings and other indescribable humiliations. I discovered too that the plighted word of the Prime Minister to the Mussulmans of India regarding the integrity of Turkey and the holy places of Islam was not likely to be fulfilled. But in spite of the foreboding and the grave warnings of friends, at the Amritsar Congress in 1919 I fought for co-operation and working the Montagu-Chelmsford reforms, hoping that the Prime Minister would redeem his promise to the Indian Mussulmans, that the Punjab wound would be healed and that the reforms inadequate and unsatisfactory though they were, marked a new era of hope in the life of India

But all that hope was shattered. The Khilafat promise was not to be redeemed. The Punjab crime was white-washed and most culprits went not only unpunished but remained in service and some continued to draw pensions from the Indian revenue, and in some cases were rewarded. I saw too that not only did the reforms not mark a change of heart, but they were only a method of further draining India of her wealth and of prolonging her servitude.

I came reluctantly to the conclusion that the British connection had made India more helpless than she ever was before, politically and economically. A disarmed India has no power of resistance against any aggressor if she wanted to engage in an armed conflict with him. So much is this the case that some of our best men consider that India must take generations before she can achieve the Dominion status. She has become so poor that she has little power of resisting famines. Before the British advent India spun and wove in her millions of cottages just the supplement she needed for adding to her meagre agricultural resources. The cottage industry, so vital for India's existence, has been ruined by incredibly heartless and inhuman processes as described by English witnesses. Little do town-dwellers know how the semi-starved masses of Indians are slowly sinking to lifelessness. Little do they know that their miserable comfort represents the brokerage they get for the work they do for the foreign exploiter, that the profits and the brokerage are sucked from the masses. Little do they realise that the Government established by law in British India is carried on for this exploitation of the masses. No sophistry, no jugglery in figures can explain away the evidence the skeletons in many villages present to the naked eye. I have no doubt whatsoever that both England and the town-dwellers of India will have to answer, if there is a God above, for this crime against humanity which is perhaps unequalled in history. The law itself in this country has been used to serve the foreign exploiter. My unbiassed examination of the Punjab Martial Law cases has led me to believe that at least ninety-five per cent of convictions were wholly bad. My experience of political cases in India leads me to the conclusion that in nine out of every ten the condemned men were totally innocent. Their crime consisted in love of their country. In ninety-nine cases out of hundred justice has been denied to Indians as against Europeans in the Court of India. This is not an exaggerated picture. It is the experience of almost every Indian who has had anything to do with such cases. In my opinion the administration of the law is thus prostituted consciously or unconsciously for the benefit of the exploiter.

The greatest misfortune is that Englishmen and their Indian associates in the administration of the country do not know that they are engaged in the crime I have attempted to describe. I am satisfied that many English and Indian officials honestly believe that they are administering one of the best systems devised in the world and that India is making steady though slow progress. They do not know that a subtle but effective system of terrorism and an organised display of force on the one hand and the deprivation of all powers of retaliation or self-defence on the other have emasculated the people and induced in them the habit of simulation. This awful habit has added to the ignorance and the self-deception of the administrators. Section 124-A under which I am happily charged is perhaps the prince among the political sections of the Indian Penal Code designed to suppress the liberty of the citizen. Affection cannot be manufactured or regulated by law. If one has no affection for a person or thing one should be free to give the fullest expression to his disaffectien so long as he does not contemplate, promote or incite to violence. But the section under which Mr. Banker and I are charged is one under which mere promotion of disaffection is a crime. I have studied some of the cases tried under it, and I know that some of the most loved of India's patriots have been convicted under it. I consider it a privilege therefore, to be charged under it. I have endeavoured to give in their briefest outline the reasons for my disaffection. I have no personal ill-will against any single admisistrator, much less can I have any disaffection towards the King's person. But I hold it to be a virtue to be disaffected towards a Government which in its totality has done more harm to India than any previous system. India is less manly under the British rule than she ever was before. Holding such a belief, I consider it to be a sin to have affection for the system. And it has been a precious privilege for me to be able to write what I have in the various articles tendered in evidence against me.

In fact I believe that I have rendered a service to India and England by showing in non-co-operation the way out of the unnatural state in which both are living. In my humble opinion, non-co-operation with evil is as much a duty as is co-operation with good. But in the past, non-co-operation has been deliberately expressed in voiolence to the evildoer. I am endeavouring to show to my countrymen that violent non-co-operation only multiplies evil and that as evil can only be sustained by violence. withdrawal of support of evil requires complete abstention from violence. Non-violence implies voluntary submission to the penalty for non-co-operation with evil. I am here, therefore, to invite and submit cheerfully to the highest penalty that can be inflicted upon me for what in law is a deliberate crime and what appears to me to be the highest duty of a citizen. The only course open to you, the Judge and the Assessors, is either to resign your posts and thus dissociate yourselves from evil if you feel that the law you are called upon to administer is an evil and that in reality I am innocent, or to inflict on me the severest penalty if you believe that the system and the law you are assisting to administer are good for the people of this country and that my activity is therefore injurious to the public weal.

M. K. GANDHI.

APPENDIX XXII

List of riots or Disturbances since the year 1919.

Province.	Date.	Place of disturbance.	Brief description.
Bombay	26th May 1919.	Godhra, Panch Mahals.	A leading wealthy member of the Gandhi community was celebrating the marriages of some of his sons and nephews. It appears that feeling was running high between the two sections of the community as some of the brides had previously been betrothed or promised to persons of the other party. The trouble began when one of the party let off potash bombs. The Gandhis then began to assemble and an altercation ensued which ended in a fight in which broken bricks and pieces of wood were freely used. The police on the spot finding that the fracas became serious, had to resort to firing. On arrival of more police, the crowd dispersed. The District Magistrate succeeded in getting both the parties reconciled to each other.

			Two rioters were injured; six policemen received injuries from bricks.
Bombay	11th June 1919	Deesa Cantonment.	Some military sepoys on duty purchased liquor, and when the police constable on duty demanded the name of the purchaser in accordance with the Cantonment Magistrate's orders, they refused to give the name and beat the constable. When one sepoy was arrested, the others interfered and attacked the constable. Three sepoys were then arrested and put in the lock up. The Sub-Inspector of Police persuaded about 200 of the men to leave the bazaar but not before the lock up was broken, the prisoners released and several policemen were injured.
			Six policemen were injured, two of them being in a serious condition.
Do.	18th June 1919.	Kanoda, Panch Mahals.	One Sania Dipsing of Kanoda was terrorizing the neighbourhood, committing robbery, frequently though mostly of trivial articles When warrants were issued for his and his brothers arrest he openly defied the authorities and even threatened to kill the police

Province.	Date.	Place of disturbance.	Brief description
			or anyone who tried to arrest him with a *dharaia*. As he could not be persuaded to surrender the District Magistrate ordered the arrest of the brothers, by using force if necessary. Senia's brothers and parents all armed with *dharaia*, clubs and pickaxes, and Sania armed with a gun resisted the arrest. The police were compelled to fire in self-defence with fatal results.
			Sania's mother and two brothers were killed. Sania himself was wounded.
Madras	22nd September 1919	Nellore.	In an attempt to enforce a decree obtained in the civil court the Hindus with police protection took a procession with music through the main bazar where there are mosques. They and the police were attached by the Muhammadans and the police compelled to fire.
			Two Muhammadens killed and two wounded.

Bombay	20th January 1920.	Bombay.	Abnormal conditions in Bombay due to general strike of mill-hands and other industrial unrest.
			One striker killed. One seriously wounded, 8 policemen, 1 police officer, 1 lorry driver and a Magistrate injured. One private individual killed and one woman injured by strikers stoning trams.
Do.	26th January 1920.	Do.	Renewed attack made by strikers, police were compelled to fire.
			One striker was wounded.
Do.	30th January 1920.	Nandvaji village Bijapur district	A police party was engaged in protecting a faction in the village against the attacks of the rival faction when it found itself in the presence of a large body of rioters with sticks, axes and stones and fearing attack on themselves the police fired two shots in the air and one on the men in front. Three wounded.
Do.	16th February 1920.	Sholapur.	During the strike of mill-hands at Sholapur some 8,000 mill—hands who had struck work surrounded

Province	Date	Place of disturbance.	Brief description
			the District Magistrate and refused to disperse when ordered to do so, by the District Magistrate. They became violont and began to stone officers and troops. The District Magistrate was compelled to order firing. It was only after the military arrived that the disturbance ceased.
			Four killed. Huzur Deputy Commissioner was injured.
Bihar and Orissa.	15th March 1920.	Jamshedpur.	A general strike of the workers at the Tata iron and steel Works, Jamshedpur began on the 24th February and continued for nearly a month. As the strike proceeded, the attitude of the strikers grew more hostile, those men who wished to work were intimidated, the gates of the works were picketted and the guards at the gates more than once stoned. The local Government despatched a large body of armed and military police to the

			spot for the protection of life and property and were compelled also to obtain assistance of regular British troops from Calcutta. On the 15th March the strikers obstructed the railway lines between the works and Tatanagar Railway station and made a most determined attack on the armed police sent out to clear the obstruction. The police were compelled to fire in self-defence and to fall back towards the works.	Killed 5, wounded 23.
Bombay.	14th April 1920	Jalalani Na-Wabshah	A fiacas took place in the Hur Criminal Tribes settlement of Jalalai Nawabshah, Sind, in the course of which one Fatu Mari was attacked by a number of Hurs who belaboured him with lathis and blows As his wife was in danger a Sub-Inspector ordered the mob to stop. The crowd made an attempt to attack the Sub-Inspector who finding his own life in danger ordered firing in self-defence and also with the object of quelling the di turbance,	Six wounded.

Province.	Date.	Place of disturbance.	Brief description.
Madras.	April 1920	Perungama nallur, Madura distt.	The attempt to register the kallars under Criminal Tribes Act brought about a serious collision between them and the police. On account of their defiant and aggressive attitude, the police had to open fire. Eleven killed.
Do.	May 1920	Muthupet in Tanjore district.	A Hindu marriage procession passing a mosque came into conflict with the Muhammadans. A fight ensued and to clear the street the police had to open fire. One man was slightly wounded.
Do.	17th May 1220.	Madras.	During a strike in the Burma Oil Company some Pathans were brought from Bambay to carry on the work. An altercation between them and the local coolies resulted in a riot which required the presence of the armed police reserve to quell it.

			One Pathan was killed; there was also minor casualties on both sides.
Bombay.	29th May 1920	Dubar Sukkur District.	On 29th May an affray took place between the police and certain Jagiranis near Durbar in the Sukkur district, Sind. The police received a complaint that two buffaloes had been stolen by some Jagiranis. A Police party went in search of the criminals and having found them seized and arrested the offenders. On their return journey they were attacked by about 30 Jagiranis two of whom were armed with guns. Those guns were fired at the police party and the Jagiranis closed in with their *lathis* A general free fight ensued and the police seeing that they were overwhelmed by weight of numbers, fired in self. defence. The Jagiranis then ran off, leaving their wounded.
			One killed, one wounded, also five policmen injured
North-West Frontier Province.	8th July 1920.	Kachagarhi.	At Kachagarhi a collision occurred between troops and Muhajarins.
			Killed one Muhajir.

Province.	Date.	Place of disturbance.	Brief description.
Punjab	25th August 1920.	Kasur	The Khilafat party asked a theatrical company to give the proceeds of their last performance to the Khilafat Fund. The company declined and was attacked at night. The police arrived on the Scene and used fire-arms.
			Ond killed and two wounded.
United Provinces.	23rd September 1920.	Pilibhit.	During the Muharram festival an attack was made on a Hindu temple at Pilibhit. The police fired a few rounds in the air.
			One wounded who subsequently died.
Madras	9th December 1920	Madras	Buckingham Mills. Perambur. The police lorry which was taking the coolies from the mills to the harbour was subjected to persistant and violent stoning by strikers. The police opened fire.
			Sixteen persons were wounded, two of whom died

List of riots or Disturbances and disturbances since the year 1921.

Province.	Date.	Place of disturbance.	Brief description.
United Provinces	7th January 1921	Rae Berilli Distt.	Agrarian disturbances in Rae Bareilly and Fyzabad Districts accompanied by extensive looting.
United Provinces	24th Jaunary 1921	...	District Rae Barielly. Police party besieged in a house after one of their number was killed.
Punjab	26th Jauuary 1921	Tarn	Serious riot at Tarn Taran. Killed... ... ... 3 Wounded 14
Bombay	9th January 1921	Kolaba Distt.	A riot occurred between two parties of Muhammadans in the Kolaba district during the course of a flag procession. The sub-Inspentor of Police

Province.	Date.	Place of distrubance.	Brief description.
			who was in charge lost his head and fired in the air. No casualities.
United Provinces	29th January 1921	Goshaingunj Railway Station, Fyzabad Distt	A large crowd held up a train with the object of rescuing a man arrested for his complicity in the agrarian riots. The police who were attacked, fired wounding one man, several others were hit with stray pellets.
			One rioter wounded,
Bengal	4th February 1921 5th February 1921	Naihati	An affray took place between a Muhammadan and a Gurkha Durwan of a Jute Mill resulting in a General fracas between Muhammadan coolies of the Mill and Gurkha durwans in which a few Gurkhas were killed and other injured It was considered doubtful whether there was any political significance.
Bihar and Orissa	7th February 1921	Giridih	Strikes at the East India Railway Colliery, Giridih, District Hazaribagh, Bihar and Orissa.

United Provinces	10th February 1921	...	Strike on the Oudh and Rohilkhand Railway, Punjab Mail stoned and Magistrate assaulted.
Bengal	18th February 1921	Calcutta	Riot in Kalighat section of Calcutta Tramway by strikers.
Bihar and Orissa	18th February 1921	Saran	District Sarat, Bihar and Orissa. Police while investigating complaint against locally self-constituted panchayet were assaulted.
Punjab	19th—20th February 1921	Nankana	Nankana Sahib affair in Punjab.
Central Provinces	21st—25th February 1921	Nagpur	Disturbances of Nagpur arising out of temperance compaign of non-co-operators.
Bengal	March 1921	Lillooah	Strike accompanied by rioting at Lillooah workshops.
Bombay	March 1921	Karachi	Hartal at Karachi accompanied by violence of mob.
Central Province	March 1921	Nagpur	Rioting during excise sales. Five liquor shops Cracked.

Province.	Date.	Place of disiturbance.	Brief description.
			Mob fired on by police, one policeman killed and 15 injured, 9 rioters killed and 14 wounded.
United Provinces	20th and 21st March 1921	Karhaiya, Rae Barelli District.	In the course of the riots which took place on the 20th March, the police were compelled to fire on two occasions. The riot started by the arrest of two men who had been prohibited from speaking and who were haranguing the crowd. Killed ... ... 4 Wounded 12
Assam	21st March 1921	...	Halem Tea Estate, Assam. Strike by tea garden labourers who assaulted officials of tea garden.
Bengal	24-3-1921	Rajshahi	Outbreak in Rajshahi Jail in Bengal.
Madras	3rd April 1921	Kumbakonam	Riots at Kumbakonam due to labour strikes.

Punjab	6th April 1921	Kamalia	Riot at Kamalia, Montgomery District, Punjab, owing to dispute over Prem Sati Gurdwara.
Bengal	15th April 1921	Ghusuri	Ghusuri Jute Mill Bengal. Riot accompanied by violence; manager seriously injured
Bombay	19th April 1921	Shikarpur	Riot at Shikarpur, Bombay, when non-co-operators interfered with yearly meeting of Pritman Dharma Sahha.
Bihar and Orissa	25th April 1921	Giridih	Owing to trial of a non-co-operation volunteer, 10,000 people at Giridhi, District Hazaribagh, endeavoured to storm sub-jail, looted police station and burnt records.
Bombay	25th April 1921	Malegaon	Disturbances at Malegaon, Bombay, arising out of trial of Khilafat, Volunteers. Sub-Inspector of Police and four constables Killed.
Madras	26th April 1921	Ottapalam	Disturbance at Ottapalam, Madras; fight between Reserve Police and khilafat volunteers.
Bihar and Orissa	May 1921	Sitamarhi	S. D. O, Sitamarhi, (District Muzuffarpur, Bihar and Orissa) compelled to leave Mela; public intimidated.

Province.	Date.	Place of disturbance.	Brief description.
Bengal	11th May 1921	Kanchrapara	Riot in Kanchrapara workshops, Eastern Bengal State Railway. Several thousands took part in riot caused by strikers of Eastern Bengal State Railway workshops, Kanchrapara.
Bengal	16th May 1921	Kaloj Valley	Riot accompanied with violence occurred at Kaloj Valley Tea State, Darjeeling District.
Assam	19th-20th May 1921	Chandpur	Trouble at Chandpur in connection with tea garden labourers leaving Assam.
United Provinces.	22nd May 1921	Mahagaon	Serious affray in Mahagaon, District Allahabad.
Bombay	26th June 1921	Bombay	Disturbances at Tata Mills Limited, Dadar, Bombay.
Bombay	1st July 1921	Dharwar	Riots at Dharwar, Bombay, arising from liquor shop picketting.

Madras	July 1921.	Madras	Strikes in Buckingham and Karnatic Mills, Madras, began accompanied by wide-spread arson.
United Provinces.	5th July 1921	Aligarh	Riot at Aligarh arising out of trial of a non-co-operators.
United Provinces.	13th July 1921	Bariha	Serious riot at Bariha village, District Lucknow.
Bengal	July 1921	Chittagong	Disturbances and disorders occurred in Bengal, both in Calcutta and at Chittagong, during trial of non-co-operators.
Bombay	21st July 1921.	Matiari	Disturbances at Matiari arising out of interference by non-co-operators with an Aman Sabha meeting.
Bombay	July 1921.	Karachi	Picketting of liquor shops at Karachi caused cases of obstruction and assault; one leading agitator rescued by crowd from police; when convicted mob threw stones at Police and passers by; various Europeans and Indians were hurt.
Bengal	1st August 1921	Jamalpur	Riot at Jamalpur workshops of the East Indian Railway resulting from *hartal*.

Province.	Date.	Place of disturbance.	Brief description.
Bombay	1st August 1921	Karachi.	Two British soldiers had an altercation with a Musalman in a hotel and when they came out were assaulted by a mob. One soldier was severely injured. The afiray was not due to political feelings.
Bombay	17th August 1921	Bombay.	Some 7,300 employees of the Great Indian Peninsula Railway Workshops at Parel demanded increased wages struck work. They stoned the time-keeper's office and afterwards set it on fire together with the records; the office of the workshops' Manager was also wrecked Some members of the Auxiliary Force who were employed in the Works succeeded in quelling the riot and dispersing the mob.
	22nd August 1921		One man was wounded in the thigh with a bayonet.
Do.	25th August 1921	...	Strikes in the Jacob and E. D. Sassoon Mills. This terminated on 8th and 12th September.

United Province,	September 1921	Kailana Chakrata U. P.	There was an affray between police and British soldiers. A Sub-Inspector and a British officer were killed. All the British soldiers and officers were tried and were acquitted.
Madras City	5th October 1921	...	A serious riot occurred between the Hindus and the Anti-Dravidas which necessitated the opening of fire by the police. The Anti-Dravidas were responsible for insulting a Muhammadan funeral procession, and attacking a Hindu procession.
Beneres	October 1921	...	An attempt made by a sub-inspector to search a cloth-shop in the village whereupon a disturbance arose and he ordered his escort to fire in the air. The Ahirs concerned seized the opportunity to attack police whilst their guns were empty. The police fled, the sub-inspector as far as Meerut. A second sub-inspector came to the rescue. A melee ensued in which a constable was killed by a lathi blow; two villagers were wounded by gun-shot wounds.

Province.	Date.	Place of disturbance.	Brief description.
Darrang District, Assam	14th October 1921.	...	Strike of tea garden coolies. The European Managers as well as the Superintendent of Police were assaulted and some of the Indian members of the garden staff were injured. Fifty-two arrests were made.
Ahmedabad	26th October 1921.	Bombay.	Thirty.one out of 47 mills closed down demanding higher wages; but this soon ended.
Bengal	26th October 1921.	Chitagong,	The conviction of Mr. J. N. Gupta on a charge of picketing led to a slight disturbance on his way to the Jail. A crowd gathered and assaulted the Gurkha Guard who dispersed them and assaulted butts of their rifles.
Bengal	24th October 1921.	Calcutta.	Two persons wearing Khilafat badges were arrested. They resisted the Police. A crowd quickly gathered. A number of arrests were made the men being conducted to the police station amidst a shower of brickbats.

Bengal	25th October 1921.	Calcutta	Strike of tramway employees.
Bihar and Orissa	October 1921	Champaran	Serious trouble occurred at Bagaha Police Station, West Champaran, the Chatawar Factory was burnt down and three persons were killed.
Punjab	30th October 1921	Lahore	On the afternoon of the 30th October 1921 a mob of between 150 and 200 convicts made a determined and evidently a preconcerted attempt to break out of the Lahore Central Jail. They overpowered the guard of the inner gate and forced their way to the outer gate where they succeeded in breaking the lock of the wicket.
			The Jail officials had to fire at this point and succeeded in driving back the convicts. Three of the convicts were killed and thirty-three wounded-
Bengal	4th November 1921	Howrah	Processions were formed at night after a Khilafat meeting had been held on the Howrah maidan. One of these attacked the police on duty and forced them

Province.	Date.	Place of disturbance.	Brief description.
			to retire on the thana. Armed police were requisitioned from Sibpore and, though attacked *en route*, succeeded in relieving the thana. During the disturbances some shots were fired.
			One constable was killed and several wounded. Five rioters were killed.
Bengal	November 1921	Bogra	An attempt was made to withhold food supplies from the Settlement Officer, Mr. Mc Pherson who was assaulted when he visited the *hat* for the purpose.
Bengal	4th November 1922	Calcutta	A serious riot occurred in Howrah Town after a Khilafat meeting when processions were formed. One of these attacked the Police who retired to the thana Armed police were requisitioned from Sibpore and were attacked *en route*. They, however, succeeded in relieving the thana. Some shots were fired by the Police and two rifles were lost. One con-

			stable was killed and several were wounded and whilst the Assistant Magistrate was injured on the head.
Bengal	14th November 1921	Calcutta	An attempt was made to renew the tramway service in Shambazar with the result that a serious disturbance occurred at the Balgachia Depot. The police force being insufficient, the military were summoned but before this the Assistant Commissioner of Police Mr. Bartley was seriously assaulted and about 20 police injured and so were several rioters.
Coorg	17th November 1921	Bangalore	Following on arrest of six Mahomedans on charge of unlawful assembly a mob numbering thousands surrounded Broadway Police station, prevented removal of prisoners who had refused bail to judicial lock-up in Bangalore Central Jail. As Police force was inadequate, military aid was requisitioned. As detachment of military reached Police station, determined rush was made on rear. In the melee four or five shots were fired. Officer Commanding was individually attacked by man with a stick. There was heavy stone throwing.

Province.	Date.	Place of disturbance.	Brief description.
			Two rioters were killed and six injured ; 16 men of the Dorset Regiment were injured.
Burma	17th November 1921	Rangoon	Serious riot occurred on 13th night due to attempt by large number of Burmese monks to obtain free entrance to the Pwes in Shwedagon Pagoda during pagoda festival.
			Not known. One unknown Burman killed. Among the police there were three serious and many minor casualties.
Bombay.	17th November '21 to 20th November 1921	Bombay	People returning from seeing the arrival of the Prince were molested. On 18th rioting became general. Europeans and Parsis were attaeked and liquor shops, etc, were set on fire. Military aid was requisitioned.
			Two Europeans, one American and two Parsis

			were killed. Three Europeans and an unknown number of Parsis were wounded. Eighty-three police were wounded. Of the rioters 53 were killed and 298 wounded. Not all the deaths from gunshot wounds were due to the police and military, as several dead and wounded men were found in localities where the authorities had not opened fire.
Madras	4th December 1921.	Cannanore	On the 4th December 1921, a number of Moplah-convicts and under-trial prisoners in the Cannanore Central Jail, ultimately numbering about 150, began rioting and attempted to break out of the Jail. Breaking open a tool shed they armed themselves with chisels, iron bars, etc., and attacked warders who attempted to obstruct their escape. As the prisoners disregarded warnings, firing had to be ordered to prevent their overpowering the guard by force of number. Seven of the prisoners were killed outright and four wounded by the firing. Two of these

Province.	Date.	Place of disturbance.	Brief description.
			subsequently died. One prisoner died of a fractured skull and nine were wounded otherwise than by firing.
Punjab	23rd December 1921	Fezorepur Jhirka	A determined attempt was made by a mob to rescue 12 non-co-operators who were arrested for having recourse to violence. The police were forced to fire on the 24th a large number assembled to renew the attack, but Alwar troops and Reserve Police dispersed them.
			Three rioters were killed and several wounded.
Bengal	28th December 1921	Rungpur	Owing to disturbed state of locality, thirty—two armed Police were sent to Nilphamari. A halt was made in the bazar during a rout march, and an altercation took place between a policeman and a servant of a local gentleman. A crowd speedily collected and began throwing missiles. March was continued fol-

			lowed by crowd who became increasingly menacing and broke through ranks of police. Some shots fired in the air.
			Eight policemen were injured. Eight of public were also injured.
United Provices.	29th December 1921	Bareilly	On the 30th December 21·32 inmates of Bareilly Juvenile Jail refused to work on the grounds that a certain political prisoner had been removed from their midst. (He had been sent to hospital in consequence of illness.) Owing to influence of political prisoners the youths, who numbered about 190, were completely out of hand. They broke open almirahs, took out tools, broke open locks and gates and attempted to scale walls. It was necessary to call up the armed guard and to order firing. Sixteen shots were fired, several of them in the air. None of the gunshot wounds are serious, an inquiry by District Magistrate shows that no unnecessary violence was used. (This account is taken from a communique published in the Press, as no official report has been received from the United Provinces Government.)

Province.	Date.	Place of disturbance.	Brief description.
			Eight of the prisoners were injured by gunshots mostly in the legs, and nine with batons.
Madras.	13th January 1922.	Madras.	On the occasion of the arrival of His Royal Highness the Prince of Wales in Madras there were disturbances in Madras City. An official report has not yet been received, but from accounts in the Press it appears that the excesses of the mob were such that it was necessary to call out the military and to resort to firing.
			According to Press accounts, five or six rioters were killed. Other casualities not known.
Burma	15th January 1922.	Hokyobo Kwin, near Mada village, Thingangyan.	A party of police were despatched to prevent a baffalo fight. They were attacked on arrival by a crowd of between three hundred and five hundred. The police made six arrests but the crowd attacked them with sticks, stones, and bottles and they had to let their

			prisoners go and to retreat towards the police station. Later the villagers again attacked the police and one villager cut a head constable with a *dah* on the fore-arm and attempted to seize his carbine. Another head constable came to the rescue and in the scuffle the carbine went off and the original assailant was shot in the abdomen. As villagers continued to attack, a head constable fired twice into the crowd. The police then made good their escape.
			One villager killed, two severely wounded, seven slightly wounded; one head constable cut on forearm, one head constable incised wound on head, two constables slight cuts about arms and several hit by missiles.
Bengal.	21st January 1922	Noakhali	The Superintendent of police while touring in his car was met with a shower of brick-bats and the S. D. O. was attacked by about 200 men.
Sub-division, Patna.	Do.	Sirajgung	A sub-inspector and 3 constables attempted to arrest three volunteers who were picketting some liquor shops A crowd gathered and succeeded in separating and beating the constables. The sub-inspector fled. The

Province.	Date.	Place of disturbance.	Brief description
			mob then went in search of the excise sub-inspector and having failed to find him, they looted the ganja and liquor shop. In the course of this incident one rifle was lost by the police.
			Several instances of vigorous picketting occurred in this neighbourhood through which the D. M. and Superintendent of Police decided to have a route march. They arrived at Salangahat with two head constables and 23 constables of armed police. A number of volunteers had collected here and as the Deputy Magistrate received complaints of interference several were arrested. A crowd of about 2,000 then gathered and pelted the police. Every effort was made to disperse the crowd. Eventually after the Deputy Superintendent of Police had been hit with a lathi the Magistrate ordered fire to be opened first with buck-shot, and when this proved unavailing, with ball. The crowd then dispersed leaving 4 dead and 6 wounded

Dacca District.	23rd January 1921.		Certain bad characters attacked the police in the course of effecting some arrests ; the latter fired killing one volunteer.
Titagarh Jute Mills.	26th January 1922		Three mill hands were wanted in connection with an assault on the Manager and Assistant Manager. Two arrests were made which resulted in the collection of a threatening crowd who hemed in the police against the wall of the mill. After failing to get in touch with the Sub Divisional Magistrate over the telephone the Deputy Superintendent ordered first one and then several of his men to fire. One man was killed and another died subsequenrly Altogether 40 were reported to have been wounded, seven were sent to hospital.
United Provinces.	1st February 1922	Chauri Chaura	An attempt to picket Muderwa bazar and prevent sales of fish, drugs and liquor had been frustrated by police. Also an Ahir (gowli caste) Government pensioner, who was a previous convict and had become volunteer, was called up and threatened with loss of his pension. The volunteers, determined on Saturday, that is the next bazar day,

Province	Date	Place of disturbance.	Brief description
			to forcibly picket the bazar and overawe all opposition by their numbers. The owner of the bazar is a loyal zamindar. The volunteers proceeded to the bazar through the police station grounds. They attacked the police station with kunkars and bricks Eventually the police fired in the air. The attack was renewed with greater force The mob rushed the police and they fled, some into the fields and some into the buildings. A few police must have fired on the mob in earnest, but it cannot be said whether it was before the rush or not. Buildings were set on fire and all the force there except one constable and one chaukidar, who escaped were brutally beaten to death and then burnt. Also a little boy servant of the Sub Inspector was murdered. Resistance to the mob was, I fear, badly organised. Then the mob tore up two rails on the line, cut telegraph wires and scattered.
			Twenty-one police and chaukidars killed & two rioters.

Bihar and Orissa.	3rd February 1922	Jamalpur.	Two Indian boys quarrelled in Railway Works, Jamalpur. One as result being rendered unconscious. Action taken by Railway authorities who dismissed two men did not satisfy popular demand for removal of head maistry and on 10th an attempt was made to assault him in office which was stoned. Works manager asked men in foundry either to work or leave aud as they refused to do either they were locked out on 11th and stoned men arriving. Crowd at Jamalpur was dispersed but many workmen came in by local trains from outside where trains were held up and line tampered with. District Magistrate regards situation as serious and fears sabotage. Military police arrived on evening 11th, Trouble expected 13th when shops re-open.
United Provinces	6th February 1921	Bareilly.	A defiant challenge was given this morning in the city by about, 5,000 volunteers who went out in procession despite prohibition. The processions were dispersed flags seized and the bands silenced. The volunteers and crowd rallied at the Town Hall The police seized the Congress office, tore down and burnt the flags Later a crowd which was reinforced by outside

Province.	Date.	Place of disturbance.	Brief description.
			help attempted to seize Town Hall and a charge by the police met with vollies of brickbats. The situation with the number of men available was impossible to hold.
			By the District Magistrate's orders fire was opened by the police and the attack repelled. The crowds remained hostile. With military assistance the situation in now in hand No firing was done by the military. The District Magistrate and the Superintendent of Police were wounded in the face by brickbats. So far as known two are killed and five wounded. The city is in the hands of the military. The District Magistrate personally satisfied himself that the firing was absolutely justified. Six men have been arrested including Abdul Wadeed, Trebeni Sahai, Moti Singh Vakil and Damodar Sarup. All is quiet now.

			One man killed on the spot, two since died in hospital five wounded now in hospital including one woman.
Assam	15th February 1922.	Jamunamukh	A riot occured at Jamunamukh on the 15th. Among Khilafat Volunteers and Sylhet settlers. Convicted prisoners were forcibly released and a mail train was held up by the removal of sleepers and stoned.
Do.	16th February 1922.	Sylhet	Commissioner. Surma Valley, who is in camp at Kanaighat was dispersing forbidden meeting when a large body of Lathials attacked the Police from behind. Armed Police turned to meet them when in spite of warning they came right on Commissioner who was hit on head by clods of earth and was narrowly missed with lathies. He called on the police to fire; several rounds were fired, resulting in about 8 casualties. As soon as firing stopped men swarmed back in great numbers. Police force then returned to thana. One rifle was lost. It is reported that reinforcements from Auxiliary Force stationed at Sylhet and Karimganj are porceeding to spot. Three police constables killed and three wounded.

APPENDIX XXIII

The Honourable Sir William Vincent's Speech at the Legislative Assembly, 18th January 1922

I say, Sir, from that time we have always avoided systematically and steadily any excessive severity *vis a vis* this movement, Later, there were a number of seditious speeches, including incitements to violence, particularly by Mr. Muhammad Ali and his brother, and Government were prepared to take action against them. What ensued is well known to the Members of this Assembly. There were meetings between Mr. Gandhi and His Excellency, and later Muhammad Ali and his brother offered to the public certain undertakings on which the Government withdrew the prosecutions against them. In a letter of June, 1921, addressed to Local Governments after this undertaking we indeed expressed some hope that it might be possible to reduce the number of prosecutions. We were anxious not to force the pace and although we always maintained our determination to keep order, we sought to avoid over-drastic action against the less dangerous or less violent adherents of the movement. At the same time we indicated to Local Governments that they were not to prosecute persons, the prosecution of whom might have great effect outside the province, without consulting the Government of India. In that letter, further, we invited Local Gcvernments to give certain other convicted persons the same *locus poenitentiae* which had been given to Muhammad Ali and his brother. We have throughout avoided very carefully any suggestion, any action which might create the impression that we desire to interfere with a legitimate political movement. I defy any Member of this Assembly to say otherwise. We have indeed frequently been reproached with weakness on this acoonnt. I maintain that it was not weakness but patience. At the same time, we made every effort to meet the legitimate wishes of educated opinion in this country. I have no time to-day to recapitulate all we have done but I should like to mention such matters as the compensation to persons injured in the Punjab disorders, the further review of the Punjab sentences, the Committee on the Press Act, the results of which will be before this Assembly very shortly; again, the Committee on repressive measures and the Committee to inquire into racial distinctions in criminal proceedings. In fact, there was no question that came before us in which we did not honestly seek to meet moderate Members of the Assembly in order to consolidate the moderate party into a great working power in the country for good. What has been response of Mr. Gandhi and his followers? I maintain that it has been one steady stream of sedition, one steady attempt to subvert Government, one method of promoting this object being adopted after another. Sometimes it has been the boycott of piece-goods in order to injure British trade, although Mr. Gandhi had himself I believe, at one time said that 'boycott' was a word that was entirely inconsistent with his principle of 'Ahimsa'. Later this movement took the form of attempts on the loyalty of our troops attempts on the police and there were constant incitements to disorder. These have resulted in serious outbreaks of violence in many parts of the country, the most important of which was the Moplah outbreak. Sir, there has recently been some attempt to minimise the cruelties committed by the Moplahs in Malabar. I refer in particular to the remarks of Mr. Abdul Bari and Mr. Husrat Mohani on this subject. Mr. Abdul Bari spoke of the pure spirit of the Moplahs and denied the veracity of the accounts of their atrocities. Mr. Husrat Mohani justifies them in the following words:

"At such a critical juncture when they are engaged in war against the English, their Hindu neighbours not only do not help them or observe neutrality but aid and assist the English in every possible way. They can indeed contend that, while they are fighting a defensive war for the sake of their religion and have left their houses, property and belongings, and taken refuge in the hills and jungles, it is unfair to characterise as plunder their commandeering of money, provisions and other necessities for their troops from the English and their supporters."

Many of us, however, have, I believe, some knowledge of the atrocities committed by these men, atrocities which I am certain in my mind that every Mussalman in this House deplores as deeply as I do, and they will appreciate what a misrepresentation of the facts this is. The barbarities of the Moplahs have been indefensible. I will cite one instance '*New India*' in support of what I say. Writing of a respectable Nair, an article in this paper states :

'When on the 26th he threatened other steps, the rebels forced their way into his house, dragged him out, along with his wife and two children carried them to the mosque and bathed all four and compelled them to recite verses from the Koran and dress as Moplahs. At mid-night they were led home and imprisoned. Next day the deponent's head was shaved and ten days later a certain notorious criminal (now in custody) forcibly circumcised the deponent. Three weeks later he and his family and other converts (some being Christians) escaped to Shoranur.

Sir, I am one of those who have been to Malabar, I have seen myself refugees, a thousand in one refuge, hungry, homeless, lacking clothes, and I can assure Members of this Assembly that it was a pitiable sight to see. I only mention the facts because this attempt has been made and because this rising, these acts of cruelty and murder are one of the direct results of the Khilafat movement. I do not put it (I never have put it) that Mr. Gandhi is responsible for this directly, but I do say that his supporters-his Muhammadan supporters—were the cause of this terrible loss of life. Indeed you have only got to read, Mr. Hasrat Mohani's speech to see what the character of the rising was. Now, if the Moplah outbreak had been an isolated instance of disorder, as I said in the last Session, the Government might not have been forced to take action against this non-co-operation movement. It might well have been argued that the circumstances were exceptional. But have Members of this Assembly read the report which is attached to the Repressive Measures Committee? Have they read the appendix setting out a list of 34 outbreaks of disorders of a serious character within a year? Sir, we have been told that after the declaration of policy by this Government in March last. the non-co-operation movement was dying down. I think that I am correct in making this statement; and I hope I am not misrepresenting anybody, Is there any foundation for it? Does not every Member of this Assembly know that that is absolutely inaccurate? Does not every Member here know that the movemement of disloyalty to the Crown, intended to paralyse Government, intended to subvert the administration, has been growing day by day throughout the year? Can any man here say that actually the movement was losing strength? Do not these disorders tell a different story—these outbreaks which culminated in the riots in Bombay on the 17th November? Before I come to that however, I want to deal with another point. May I inform this Assembly that, during the present year, it has been necessary to call out the military to suppress serious disorder no less than 47 times? May I tell them that, during the last three months, military assistance has had to be invoked—I have here the figures from His Excellency the Commander in-Chief—no less than 19 times? Does that look as if the forces of disorder were losing strength before the Government took this action?

And now, Sir, I want to turn to the rioting in Bombay in which the lawless tendencies of those who follow Mr. Gandhi—not of Mr. Gandhi himself—culminated. Bombay is a city in which Mr. Gandhi is supposed to exercise the greatest influence. He himself was present there on the 17th November. The occasion was one, one would have thought, when at least every loyal citizen of the Crown, whatever his political views, would have avoided any disorder or riot. It was the occasion of the landing of His Royal Highness the Prince of Wales, the heir to the Throne of England. That was the occasion chosen by the non-co-operators in Bombay for an outbreak of violence which, I believe, has not been paralleled in that city for many many years, and what was the object of those who embarked upon this campaign of violence? I say the object was vengeance, vengeance on those who dared to go forth to welcome His Royal Highness the Prince of Wales in spite of Mr. Gandhi's direction—that was the sole crime of the unfortunate people so maltreated. That Sir, is the result of non-violent non-co-operation. Was Mr. Gandhi able to exercise any influence to stop the demand? Why, it was pathetic to read his words next day. He was full of sorrow, but he had not thought of the consequences of his act before. After all he had warning on previous occasions. Well, Sir, I do not know that I need go through the events of these terrible days. You have heard from my Honourable friend, Mr. Dwaraka Das, how women were assaulted in the public streets; you have read in the papers how harmless Europeans and Indians, including many Parsis, were murdered, or assaulted, how one unfortunate engine driver, going home from his work, a harmless individual, was suddenly attacked and murdered by a cruel mob. All this was the result of this non-violent movement. The reports say that it began in intimidation and that was not checked, those who had been guilty of intimidation thought they could proceed with impunity to violence. The damage done to property also—the property of private individuals—was very great. I read in one report, of 137 shops being looted and that is an under statement of all the damage.

Now, let us see what was happening in other places on that day? In Delhi there was *hartal* enforced by systematic threats and intimidation. And I assert here, and I dare any one to contradict me, that intimidation was practised by men posing as volunteers; men dressed as volunteers who paraded the streets and interfered with the liberty of law-abiding citizens in a manner that is intolerable in any civilised community. Is it surprising that we received many complaints actually of absolute want of any Government control at the time? In Calcutta, again there was *hartal* promoted by general intimidation and violence on the part of volunteers. It is idle for any one to deny it. Mr. Abdul Kasem and other Members were in Calcutta and they know the facts. The Government of Bengal, writing on the 26th November, reported that an incessant stream of seditious speeches was being poured forth, that money was being freely spent in the employment of paid agents; and here I may tell the Assembly that many of these volunteers,—I do not say all of them because that would be wrong,—

—but many of these volunteers are merely paid men, paid a rupee a day, and, in fact when the supply of money dries up,—and there have been places where this has happened,—the supply of volunteers has run short. We were also told by the Bengal Government that on the 17th there was general suspension of activities of all kinds and the riff-raff of the city, under the gui e of volunteers, was abroad, terrorising and absuing law-abiding folk, and there were numerous instances of molestations of Europeans and Indians. The authority of Government was openly flouted; and law abiding citizens were depressed because of Government's failure to protect them, I have got instances here of the different kinds of speeches made in Bengal. I do not think I need cite them except to mention that one of them says :

'That the Bengalees had discovered the death-arrow of the English. Remember Kanai and Khudiram Bose and others of Bengal.'

I do not suppose the Members of this Assembly know, who they were ; they were prominent murderers ; some, if not all of them, were hanged. Well, Sir, the whole effect of the activities was that, on the 17th of November in Calcutta there was an absolute effacement of the authority of Government, and general intimidation throughout the whole of the city. I am told now that we exaggerated all this : There was a *hartal*, it is true, but there was nothing more than a voluntary one. Well, the *Amrita Bazar Patrika*, itself stated on the morning of the 18th a most significant fact—I cite it because it is testimony coming from an adversary—it said on the 18th 'Writ large on the *hartal* of Calcutta is revolution'. Now I ask the Assembly to ponder those words.

I may say that throughout all this period the most desperate efforts were made to create racial animosity. Those who were in Calcutta in December last—I was there know how true this is and it was a very dangerous factor in the situation. There was also at that time every reason to believe that if the activities of these so-called volunteers were not curtailed, we should have a repetition in Calcutta of what we had in Bombay. Now the total deaths is Bombay were 53 people killed, and I think something like 400 injured went to the Hospital. The problem before the Government, therefore, was : are you going to sit quietly, or, as my Honourab'e friend said, ' with folded hands' and watch with apathy and inertia this slaughter of innocent people, or are you going to take action while there is yet time? The Assembly remember also that previously, on the 14th of November, there had been already a dangerous riot in Calcutta at Belgatchia, in which over 5,000 people had been engaged. Now, I maintain that, in such circumstances, the Bengal Government were fully justified in taking the action. We have abundant testimony that, whatever be the professions of those who inaugurate these volunteer movement, their practice and precept are poles apart. You may say that they enter into a solemn vow of non-violence, but in practice they are repeatedly constantly and persistently, guilty of intimidation and violence. Let me turn to another province. I have got a report here from the Bihar Government. We called for these reports to see on what grounds they had proceeded against these associations. The replies show that Local Governments were satisfied that the members of the proscribed associations went in systematically for this class of offence. To return to Bihar, on the 10th of December, I received a report from the Local Government which says that these volunteers had been guilty of intimidation, violence and other forms of criminal action on no loss than 122 occasians reported in the last year. One of the incidents is worthy of special mention, indeed many of them are. The one to which I refer was the case of a poor Muhammadan who had the misfortune to be a law-abiding subject of the Crown. He died in Ranchi and his funeral had to be performed. But the non-co-operators said : 'No, he shall not be buried by Muhammadans." Well, some over-daruni spirit said : 'Oh, his was not so great an offence that we should allow this oppression ; men who differ from other in their political views are entitled to a little toleration.' So they took the body to the graveyard with police protection and buried it. What was the next action of the extremists? The non-co-operation volunteers dug up the corpse and dishonoured it, ('Shame.') Well that is the conduct of these non-violent non-co-operation volunteers. Again, on the 17th, in Calcutta, there were unfortunately two Muhammadans who died in Ballygunge of natural causes and those who wished to bury them could not procure the necessary assistance; they were unable to procure bearers or *Khatias* or anything else and the bodies remained unburied foi the whole of that day. There was many a sick man and woman in Calcutta on the 17th who could not procure medical attendance. No conveyances for medical practitioners, and when doctors walked to the patients and attended on them, they wonld not get medicine. because the dispensaries were not allowed under the strict orders of the non-co-operators to sell medicine even to save life on that day. Now, is that intimida-iton or is it not? I have been told that Government interferes with the liberty of the subject in proscribing these associations. I am amazed at the audacity of those who make such an accusation, whether it comes from the Members of this Assembly or from those who are of different political opinions, and I inclnde Mr Gandhi. Who in reality has interfered with the liberty of the subject to the same extent as members of his party? Who is it that will not allow those who wish to welcome the Prince to do so? Who prevents reasonable respect being shown to the dead! Who boycots and intimidates those who venture to serve the Crown or wish to sell or buy foreign piece-goods? Who will not allow any member of the Assembly to address a pnblic meeting without interruption? ('Hear, hear',) Who, then; is it that is really guilty of interference with the liberty of the subject? What extremist can make, with justice, this accusation against the Gov-ment? What has the Government done in this matter? * * *

And now, Sir, I wish to turn to our instructions of 24th Nov-ember, in so far as the Criminal Law Amendment Act goes. They were to the effect that where associations practised intimidation violence and obstruction, it was necessary to suppress those activi-ties and that the Act of 1908 should be used for that purpose. I believe, up to a certain point at any rate, it has been succesful. What followed? A number of young men—many of them in

Calcutta, hired from the mills—joined these associations as volunteers for a money reward. Many are doing it in Delhi now and a rupee a day is the price. They join the volunteers in defiance of all orders and then complain bitterly and pose as patriots, if they are arrested. In Delhi, when the movement first started and arrests took place, the authorities were anxious not to impose too severe penalties on accused and the consequence was, they were sentenced simple imprisonment. Many of them were quite pleased; they were able to get free meals and had nothing to do, so later it was found necessary to sentence others to rigorous imprisonment. At once there was a general feeling that this was very unfair, though it was really a very natural consequence, Throughout, however, the Government have been very anxious to avoid any appearance of undue severity; to avoid any appearance of unreasonable harshness we have made various suggestions to the Local Governments with which I will deal later. Apart from this, however, His Excellency was never unmindful of the dangers of a purely repressive policy and, as every Honourable Member knows he received a deputation on the 21st December in Calcutta and listened to their views on the action of Government and the possibility of a conference between different sections of the community and Government. And I should like to read to Honourable Members one or two words from His Excellency's reply to that deputation because, to my mind, his words breathe a lofty tone of statesmenship and indicate a deep desire to find a solution of the problem of all the difficulties with which the Government are faced. He spoke words over which every Member of this Assembly would do well to ponder. Referring to a suggestion that Government should cease making use of measures now enforced and release prisoners convicted under the law, he said:

'I cannot believe that this was the intention, of the deputation, when originally suggested, for it would mean that throughout the country intimidation and unlawful oppression and other unlawful acts should be allowed to continue, whilst Government action maintain order and protect the law-abiding citizen would be largely paralysed. I need scarcely tell you that no responsible Government could even contemplate the acceptance of such a state of public affairs. I wish with all my heart, that it had been possible to deal with these problems in a large and generous spirit, worthy of such on occasion in the history of India. Had there been indications to this effect before me to-day in the representations which you have made in your address on the part of the leaders of non-co-operation, had the offer been made to discontinue open breaches of thelaw for the purpose of providing a calmer atmosphere for discussion of remedies suggestad, my Government would never have been backward in response. We would have been prepared to consider the new situation in the same large and generous spirit I would have conferred with Local Governments for this purpose.

Sir, now what was Mr. Gandhi's reply to this? This is what Mr. Gandhi said;

'I am sorry that I suspect Lord Reading of complicity in the plot to unman India.'

I would ask Honourable Members of this Assembly if they would take that view. He proceeded to say:

"I am forced to conclude that Lord Reading is trying to emasculate India by forcibly making free speech and popular organization impossible."

In another article he said:

'I was totally unprepared for what I most respectfully call his mischievous misrepresentation of the attitude of the Congress and the Khilafat organisations in connection with the visit of His Royal Highness the Prince of Wales.

This country is, in truth, faced with a very grave crisis; we have civil disobedience looming before us. We have threats of organised violence from an influential section of the Mussalman population. We have had outbreaks of violence of a dangerous character showing what may happen in a more extended degree in future. We have had the most terrible bloodshed and loss of life. We are face to face with a situation in which there may be, I fear, greater loss of life and greater bloodshed. It is for the Assembly to say whether they are now going to encourage the forces which make for ruin and disorder. It is for them to say whether, consistently with their oath of allegiance to the Crown, most solemnly sworn here, they can conscientiously and deliberately encourage those who intend to overthrow this Government by any means that is possible. Lastly, it is for them to ponder their responsibility not only to the Assembly, not only to the Government and to the country, but also to themselves. It is for them to say whether they will take such a course as will facilitate a real and very grave danger to their own properties, to their own lives to their own honour.

THE TATA PRINTING WORKS, 5, THAMBU CHETTY ST., MADRAS.